Twayne's United States Authors Series

SYLVIA E. BOWMAN, *Editor*

INDIANA UNIVERSITY

Henry George

HENRY GEORGE

By EDWARD J. ROSE

University of Alberta
(Canada)

Twayne Publishers, Inc.   ::   New York

Preface

WAS Henry George the most important and most influential spokesman we have had for the non-Marxist left? Did he proclaim a pragmatic program in order to realize the American Dream? Was he a world-famous writer in his own time? We should be wrong if we said no to any of these questions. There was a time, not long ago, when Henry George's name was a household word. Once known to men in every walk of life, Henry George has now passed into relative obscurity, despite the school founded in his name and dedicated to the teaching of his ideas. Since he is largely unknown to many whose liberal and general education should have made them at least superficially aware of his extremely important role in the literature and social or political economics of the closing decades of the nineteenth century and the early years of the twentieth, it may be difficult for many people to accept the late President Franklin Delano Roosevelt's statement that George was "one of the really great thinkers produced by our country."

The popularity of George's major work, *Progress and Poverty*, has been unrivaled in the whole of the literature of economics. First published late in 1879, after the post-Civil War depression of the 1870's had struck even the booming state of California, it captured almost immediately the imagination of countless people throughout the world. It is not often in any age that a book on political economy becomes a best-seller and its author an international hero, but that is exactly what *Progress and Poverty* and its author became. In contrast to the depression-ridden 1930's, our present affluence has made many of us—if not all of us—forget the problems to which Henry George addressed himself, problems perhaps more complicated and pressing than ever. The war on poverty has been reopened recently, and the irony of starvation and poverty amidst apparent world-wide progress and plenty has been recognized once again. Nearly a century ago, Henry George said he had the needed remedy.

The purpose of the following study is to reacquaint the reader with the man whom Bernard Shaw said converted him and five-sixths of his fellow British socialists to socialism—a San Francisco newspaper editor who at different stages in his career corresponded with such nineteenth-century greats as John Stuart Mill and Leo Tolstoy. In order to do justice to George, it is necessary to trace his development as a man and a writer. Like most American men of letters, George was not simply a writer of books; he was a personality, and those who touch *Progress and Poverty* touch not only a book but a man. However, he must be seen as the celebrity he was without obscuring his importance and influence as a thinker and a writer. George's place in the literature of America is his alone.

In 1927, John Dewey said that "It would require less than the fingers of the two hands to enumerate those who, from Plato down, rank with Henry George among the world's social philosophers. . . . No man, no graduate of a higher educational institution, has a right to regard himself as an educated man in social thought unless he has some first-hand acquaintance with the theoretical contribution of this great American thinker." What exactly is Henry George's "theoretical contribution" to social thought, and why did men so dissimilar as Shaw, Tolstoy, and Dewey think of him as they did? What made his theories influential and convincing? Needless to say, these questions are worthy of attention.

The plan of the present discussion is straightforward: the first chapter discusses George's origins, his early training and experience as an explorer or observer of the world and as a young newspaperman; the second examines his work and activity before the publication of *Progress and Poverty*; the third is devoted to his masterwork, its publication, form, and content, and the reaction it caused; the fourth and fifth chapters discuss his writings and political activity, after the publication of *Progress and Poverty*, until his death; and the sixth chapter attempts a short review of the legacy left behind by his person and his works.

This book is intended for the general reader and also for the specialist in American literature whose knowledge of Henry George may be slight. I attempt an explanation and evaluation of George's ideas and theories while also demonstrating that he was a writer of considerable gifts. For these reasons and because George's work is largely unread today, I have quoted frequently from both his published and unpublished writings. Like most students, scholars, and adherents of George, I realized long ago that it is almost impossible to explain George more incisively and effectively than he does himself. One characteristic that most books on George have in common is the liberality with which they quote the spoken and written words of their subject. Since George understood himself, his ability to express his economic theories with simple evangelical force was essentially his greatest gift.

While preparing this book for publication, I discovered that not only is George no longer generally known to the average man in the street or to the general reader, he is relatively unknown to graduates of higher educational institutions—John Dewey notwithstanding. After surveying several large departments of English and American literature, I learned that only a few of my colleagues had even heard of Henry George. While this may not be surprising to anyone constantly confronted with the growth and departmentalization of knowledge today, even within the same discipline, it does not explain my experience with an American teacher of American literature at an American university, whose master's essay and doctoral thesis were each devoted to American writers, who asked me in all innocence: "Who is Henry George?"

Though hostile to George in his lifetime and still apt to view him as a kind of prolix amateur, the professional social philosophers, political scientists, and economists are not, however, unaware of George. This fact has caused me to wonder continually at the ironies forever part of the Henry George saga; for George's success—as I have already implied and as I try to demonstrate in this book—was traceable to the way in which he expressed his theory as much as to the concept itself. For this reason, it is an unforgivable error to equate the whole of George's philosophy with the idea of the single tax. George was a gifted writer and a powerful speaker who was endeavoring to express a vision of man—not simply a fiscal policy. Had *Progress and Poverty* been an ordinary Victorian document, it would have scarcely outlived the year of its publication. Very few subjects are more difficult to write about entertainingly and convincingly than economic theory, and George did not use fiction as a vehicle for his ideas as did many of his contemporaries.

While I do not expect to please all Georgists by discussing

George mainly as a successful propagandist and as a writer with economic ideas rather than only as an economic theorist, I may convince students of American literature or, for that matter, students of nineteenth-century English literature to read George as they read Emerson. It is time students of literature, as well as Georgists, appreciated George the poet as much as George the prophet. Without recognizing the effectiveness of the poetry of George's prose, it is impossible to appreciate his personal vision of "The Great Society." In a nation already proud in the nineteenth century of its affluence and abundance yet unaware of, if not unconcerned with, its poverty, Henry George did his best to alert America and much of the world to the strange anomaly of poverty amidst plenty, a fact more blatantly obvious today than in George's time. In this way, his words are as timely as ever. To Georgists, as it would be to George, the latest war on poverty is only another phase in a continuing struggle.

As others have done, I should like to acknowledge my debt to Henry George's first biographer, his son and former United States congressman, Henry George, Jr. I should like to thank the Robert Schalkenbach Foundation for its help and for its permission to quote from its editions of George's work and its other publications. I am grateful, too, for the courtesy shown me by the directors of the Henry George Schools in New York and London. My thanks are due also to the New York Public Library and its staff in the Library's manuscript and economics divisions for making available to me the very fine Henry George Collection. Anyone who has ever had the opportunity of using this collection must express his appreciation of the wisdom and kindness of its principal donor, the late Anna George de Mille, Henry George's daughter. In addition, I wish to express my gratitude to the Canada Council and to the General Staff Research Fund of the University of Alberta for summer grants which materially aided my labors.

EDWARD J. ROSE

University of Alberta
Edmonton, Alberta
Canada

Acknowledgments

Grateful acknowledgment is made to the following for permission to quote from copyrighted material: to Oxford University Press for permission to quote from *Henry George* by Charles Albro Barker; to Michigan State University Press for permission to quote from *Henry George in the British Isles* by Elwood P. Lawrence; to Princeton University Press for permission to quote from *The Single Tax Movement in the United States* by Arthur N. Young; and to E. P. Dutton and Company for permission to quote from *Seventy Years of Life and Labor* by Samuel Gompers.

Contents

Chronology

1839   September 2, Henry George born in Philadelphia, the first son of Richard George.

1848   Henry George's father leaves Episcopal Church publishing firm and bookstore to return to work in the Customs House. Henry is transferred to the Episcopal Academy of Philadelphia.

1852   Henry's father begins seventeen-year term as vestryman at St. Paul's Protestant Episcopal Church. Henry leaves Episcopal Academy.

1853   On February 5, Henry enters the new Philadelphia High School; leaves on June 20; formal education ended.

1855   Henry George signs aboard the Indiaman *Hindoo* as foremast boy; leaves for a fifteen-month voyage to Australia. Keeps a sea journal.

1856   Works in Philadelphia as a printer's apprentice.

1857   Leaves for California aboard the *Shubrick* as ship's steward, December 22.

1858   Goes gold prospecting in British Columbia; returns to San Francisco "dead broke"; works as a typesetter.

1860   Becomes foreman printer on the *California Home Journal*; begins political and newspaper activities in California.

1861   Enters into partnership to buy the San Francisco *Daily Evening Journal*. December 3, marries Annie Fox.

1862   November 3, Henry George, Jr., born, the future congressman and first biographer of his father.

1865   Publishes several articles, including "Sic Semper Tyrannis!" in the *Alta California* following the assassination of Lincoln. January 27, second son, Richard Fox George, born.

1867   Becomes managing editor of the San Francisco *Times*. Third child, Jennie Teresa, born.

1868   Leaves *Times*; becomes managing editor of San Francisco *Chronicle*. Publishes "What the Railroad Will Bring Us" in the October *Overland Monthly*. Travels to Philadelphia and New York at the end of the year in the employ of the San Francisco *Herald*.

1869   Fight with Associated Press-Western Union monopoly, begins a life-long struggle against vested interests. Returns to San Francisco; works as an editor on the Oakland *Daily Transcript*; corresponds with John Stuart Mill.

1870   His Oakland "illumination" concerning land value. Becomes editor of the *State Capital Reporter* (Sacramento).

1871   Publishes in pamphlet form, *The Subsidy Question and the Democratic Party* and his first extended "Georgian" document, *Our Land and Land Policy*, based on an earlier article in the *Overland Monthly* in 1868. December 4, with two partners, begins publication of the San Francisco *Daily Evening Post*.

1875   November 27, leaves the *Post* because of financial troubles and editorial differences.

1876   Becomes State Inspector of Gas Meters, a political and intellectual reward from former Democratic State Senator William S. Irwin, the new governor of California.

1877   Lectures at the University of California; delivers oration at San Francisco's Fourth of July celebrations. Begins writing *Progress and Poverty*, September 18. October 2, fourth child, second daughter, Anna Angela, born.

1878   June, delivers lecture on "Moses" in San Francisco; often repeated in later years in the United States and United Kingdom.

1879   *Progress and Poverty* published.

1880   Returns to New York.

1881   *The Irish Land Question* published; makes first trip to England and Ireland as a representative of the *Irish World*.

1881- Thoroughly involves himself in English and Irish politics;
1882   arrested in Ireland. Visits Paris.

[16]

1882   Unknowingly converts Bernard Shaw to "Socialism." October 4, returns to New York "pretty near famous."

1883   *Social Problems* published. December 21, makes a lecture tour of the United Kingdom.

1884   April 13, returns to New York. Attacked in "The Prophet of San Francisco" by the Duke of Argyll; attack and George's rejoiner in *Nineteenth Century*. Sails for England a third time.

1886   *Protection or Free Trade* published. Runs as leader of labor for mayor of New York City.

1887   Edits *The Standard* in New York City. Runs for secretary of state in New York.

1889-   Becomes the "Father of the Single Tax."
1890

1889   Sails for England; visits Paris for the second time. Returns to continue his lecture schedule.

1890   With Mrs. George and daughters, sails from San Francisco, February 8, for Australia and New Zealand. Returns to the United States by traveling around the world. December 5, suffers a stroke.

1891   *The Condition of Labor* published, his famous open letter in reply to Pope Leo XIII's encyclical letter on the condition of labor.

1892   *A Perplexed Philosopher* published.

1894   Corresponds with Leo Tolstoy, who had admired George's views for many years.

1896   Hears William Jennings Bryan's "Cross of Gold" address. Supports Bryan for the Presidency.

1897   Against medical advice, George runs again for mayor of what was to be on January 1, 1898, the City of Greater New York. Four days before the election, October 29, Henry George dies of a stroke. The funeral procession on October 31 is compared to Abraham Lincoln's.

1898   *The Science of Political Economy*, though unfinished, published posthumously.

From Philadelphia to San Francisco: The Search for a Meaningful Role in Expanding America

HENRY GEORGE lived less than sixty years, but when he died he had become a national hero and an international celebrity. His economic and social theories had reached lands that were only metaphors to Whitman. If the American Dream was ever a reality, it was in the social philosophy of Henry George's rather transcendental political economy that it was made concrete and pragmatic. For the non-American, and for many Americans also, George's ideas were a restatement in applied economics of the meaning of the Declaration of Independence. His major works, particularly *Progress and Poverty*, influenced the economic structure of nations, such as New Zealand, Australia, and Denmark; writers, such as Shaw, Bellamy, Garland, Tolstoy, and Dewey; political figures, such as Sun Yat-sen; and political movements, such as that of the British socialists in the last twenty years of the nineteenth century.

George belonged to both Emerson's America and the ages of Jackson and Lincoln, but he proclaimed the decentralized democracy of Jefferson. In many ways Henry George is America; for, having grown up in Jacksonian and Emersonian times, he lived through the Civil War to survive its divisive effects and to mature as a thinker in an expanding America which was destined to become a world power by the end of the century.

George was born in Philadelphia on September 2, 1839; and his early life foreshadows his destiny as much as it indicates the heritage into which he was born and which sustained him throughout his life. He spoke with the ring of the Liberty Bell in his voice, born as he was within range of its sound. Bernard

Shaw said that George spoke with evangelic earnestness "of Liberty, Justice, Truth, Natural Law, and other strange eighteenth century superstitions; and . . . explained with great simplicity and sincerity the views of The Creator, who had gone completely out of fashion in London in the previous decade and had not been heard of there since. I noticed also that he was a born orator. . . ."[1]

Like Thoreau, George "travelled a good deal in Concord," for concord was what he preached and concord was what had impressed itself most clearly upon his mind and character. Of George, it could be said, "he travelled a good deal in Philadelphia."[2] The "Prophet of San Francisco," first well known in the city named for the saint who preached voluntary poverty rather than poverty amidst progress, was reared in the city in which the Continental Congress had met and in which the government of the United States was first formed, a city named for brotherly love. Like America, George went to the West to grow to maturity only; like America once again, he returned to England and Europe to preach the gospel of the New World to the Old.

I *Henry George's Early Background*

Henry George was born into a low middle-class family of English, Welsh, and Scottish ancestry that had come to America in the eighteenth century. His grandfather was a Yorkshireman who became a British seaman and later an American sea captain, so the lure and lore of the sea came to Henry George naturally. The family was pious and also active in the Episcopal Church, and Henry grew up well-tutored in the Bible and in the Anglican tradition. George came by his religious "bump of reverence"[3] as normally as he did his experiences at sea. Nurtured by an environmental and national devotion to individual rights, expressed most powerfully in the Declaration of Independence and in the Constitution and Bill of Rights, Henry George's later social theories were deeply and continually influenced by the moral perogatives of the Judaic-Christian consciousness. These three early and formative influences—travel, by sea especially; the Judeo-Christian tradition, in particular its moral, natural and supernatural views of man; and the American fight for independence, with its dedication to the republican and democratic ideals of individual liberty—had a permanent effect upon everything George experienced, thought, or wrote in later life.

Henry George, the second child and first son of Richard S. H. George, grew up in a household that steadily increased in number. Not what could be called well-to-do, the George family never was impoverished, in spite of times when some spartan measures had to be taken. Though George's father had worked for years in the Customs House, at the time of Henry's birth he operated a small bookstore and book publishing business for the Protestant Episcopal Church. The family was then in fairly comfortable means. After spending three years at Mrs. Graham's private school, Henry attended public school. In 1849, a year later, he began at the Episcopal Academy. He did not remain there long, however, and his father placed him in the hands of a tutor to prepare him for high school. Somehow Henry George never seemed satisfied or settled in a formal educational institution, no matter how excellent. In less than five months, Henry George's formal schooling ended, and his working career began. His first position was in a china and glass importing house at two dollars a week. He was still several months short of his fourteenth birthday.

Henry George may have left school for good, but he never stopped reading. And as later in life, Henry George explored the written word from the Bible to the contemporary novel. His studies, however, were not entirely free of all formal patterns of learning, even immediately after leaving high school. The variety of subjects which interested George already indicated his eclectic tastes. Besides reading at the Franklin Institute, he also attended lectures there. His experiences at the Franklin Institute were probably the most important and the most lasting. The institution, named after the archetypal American self-made man, was founded for "the promotion and encouragement of manufactures and the mechanic and useful arts"—the kind of pragmatic appeal to which George would always respond.

To the young George, however, the city's wharves were as captivating as the Franklin Institute. He was often to be found there, and he had heard already from his father the many stories of his grandfather's adventures at sea. It was now 1855, and Henry George at sixteen, in search of himself, was literally to make a passage to India. And though it would have been premature for Emerson to have written his congratulations to a callow teen-age boy making his first voyage to sea, the father-philosopher of American Transcendentalism and Walt Whitman, its self-appointed poet (that very year publishing the first of the many editions of *Leaves of Grass*), might well have been struck by the symbolic significance of the ship in which Henry George first sailed from New York harbor in April. George's voyage on the *Hindoo* was to begin a series of experiences which were to be his Yale College and his Harvard.

II *Sea Ventures*

Through the intervention of friends of the family and with his father's understanding that his son had inherited his longing for the sea, Henry George left Philadelphia for New York to set sail as foremast boy aboard the Indiaman *Hindoo*. Perhaps, his father thought, such a voyage would exorcise the spirit of the sea that for the time had inhabited his son. During his voyage before the mast, George kept a journal, a habit he had before going to sea. And though the journal was only the record of a boy's first real experiences away from home, the practice it afforded for the setting down of observations and ideas forever stood George in good stead. Despite spelling errors and variations in his hand (hardly unusual for his age and experience), there are many impressive passages, written with expression and economy, in the journal. Besides recording the routine and the disastrous events of the voyage, George was capable of capturing the beautiful. On May 28, 1856, during the return voyage, George in a quick, young, and unpunctuated hand caught the mysterious beauty of the sea:

> I witnessed this afternoon, one of the most beautiful rain showers that I have ever seen, it was about 4 p m the sun shining bright-ly the squall or rather shower came up astern the space over which it extended seemed not above ¼ mile in width & its bounds were as clearly marked on the water as those of a sandy beach, where it was raining the sea seemed as though it were molten silver which contrasted so strongly with the deep blue adjoining were [sic] the wind curling the tops of the waves made a most beautiful appearance, over the whole was suspended a small but most beautiful rainbow, the shower quickly came on us, but it was light, & as quickly departed.[4]

The *Hindoo's* arrival in Australia occasioned a rebellion of sorts on the part of the crew. The sailors planned to leave the ship as soon as possible, for the country around Melbourne had become known as a "Land of Promise, where gold was to be had by all." The incident proved in many ways to be a foreshadowing of George's future career: he was several years later—on the West Coast of the United States and Canada—to get the gold fever himself. He was witnessing clearly, perhaps for the first time, a struggle between management and labor; and, like Dana and Melville, he saw firsthand the injustice of the laws of the sea, against which he willingly renewed the struggle in San Francisco in 1873.

For several days the tension aboard the *Hindoo* increased. Finally the Captain agreed to the sailors' demand that the American Consul come aboard to hear their grievances. Sitting upon the booby hatch, "with the shipping articles before him," he interviewed the crew individually. After hearing their complaints of sickness and injury, which could be blamed on the ship's age and condition, and to the bad treatment they had received from the ship's officers—all of which George records in his journal—the Consul found in favor of the Captain. It was agreed that they would be paid and willingly discharged once the cargo of lumber was unloaded. The sailors demanded the promise be put in writing, which the Captain refused to do. Unwilling to work without a written guarantee, the striking sailors were given a month's hard labor on board a prison ship. The Captain proceeded to have the *Hindoo* unloaded at perhaps less cost than the payment of the sailors' wages from New York. Later, with the needed ballast aboard, the Captain had to ship a new crew for the remainder of the voyage to Calcutta and the return to New York. Though the Captain was George's benefactor and a friend of the George family, Henry's sympathies in the journal were clearly with the striking sailors. Henry George's first sea voyage, then almost half over, actually began a greater and longer exploration abroad the more treacherous seas of political economy and labor-management relations.

Australia proved not to be the "Land of Promise." Unemployment was widespread. When the *Hindoo* finally went on to Calcutta, Henry George was again made to face the economic facts of life, for India was even more disappointing than

Australia. In the sea journal, he writes: "one feature which is peculiar to Calcutta, was the number of dead bodies floating down [the river] in all stages of decomposition, covered by crows & bromlikites who were actively engaged in picking them to pieces, the first one I saw filled me with horror & disgust but like the natives you soon cease to pay any attention to them."[5] Poverty and starvation, and human indifference, characterized his ports of call. As one of his biographers remarks, "India was never mystic India to Henry George after his visit; it was an actual grim, and suffering India. And in course of time, when as social critic he was ready to compare people and their problems, having seen the land was to make the literature of India the more fascinating to him, and his argument the more effective."[6] America was another land of promise, like Australia, and a new India, like the rich and fabled one of old. Was its destiny to be the same? What was the relation between progress and poverty to be? Henry George was one day to investigate the economic problems that beset the West in the hope that its decline would not be like that of the East.

After fourteen months, Henry George returned home to work as an apprentice typesetter. For the time, his confrontation of the exotic was curbed by the ordinary. However, this trade eventually took him into the newspaper world in the years that were to come, an everyday vocation no less important to his future career than those exciting experiences at sea.

During a period in which the slavery issue grew more and more intense, Henry George, once again in Philadelphia, was faced with the problems of the times—low wages and property rights. Though his family was Democrat, Henry was clearly anti-slavery. It was hard for Henry George ever to believe that people could be regarded as private property, especially when one day he was to deny that land itself could be so regarded. Friction at home and on the job, uncertainty about employment, an active interest in books and friends of some radical bent, the reading of Emerson, a flirtation with Swedenborg—all contributed to Henry adolescent restlessness. He was determined to go west. Finally the opportunity presented itself. Again Henry George went to sea, receiving an appointment as ship's steward aboard the Light-House Steamer *Shubrick* through the support of Congressman Thomas B. Florence. On December 22, 1857, the

Shubrick left for the long trip down the coasts of North and South America. Though George wanted only to go to California, he had to sign the ship's articles for a full year's service.

Once again George kept a journal. The ship, after battling a severe storm off Cape Hatteras, put into St. Thomas in the Virgin Islands and then passed Barbados to Rio de Janeiro. The primary experience of the voyage took place at Montevideo. Retold later in a California sketch under the title "Dust to Dust," the incident involved the failure of a burial at sea, the coffin's mysterious reappearance by the side of the ship, and its subsequent clandestine burial in a little valley near Montevideo without the knowledge of the port officials.

After the impressive passage through the Strait of Magellan, the *Shubrick* touched at Valdivia, Valparaiso, Panama, and San Diego, and arrived at San Francisco on May 27, 1858. Henry George had come for the first time to the city in which he was to become famous and whose prophet he was later dubbed. Though his years before the mast were over, he was still to travel many thousands of miles over land and sea, often before the masthead of a newspaper and eventually flying the flag of his own light-house ship, progress without poverty—the American Dream.

III *Footloose in the West*

The eighteen-year-old young man who came to San Francisco was one who had sailed both east and west, had rounded the Cape of Good Hope and seen Tierra del Fuego, sailed the Atlantic and Indian Oceans, gazed upon the Pacific and knew the greater part of the coastal waters of the New World. He had in two trips almost traveled around the world before he was twenty. One day he was truly to travel west around the world, but that was long after he had become an international hero and a force to be reckoned with in Ireland, England, Europe, and America. Through the help of Ellen George, the wife of his California cousin James, Henry George succeeded in leaving the *Shubrick*, even though he had as yet seven months to serve. He had worked his way to California indeed, for it is clear that he never received his accumulated wages. Though his name does not appear among the deserters of the *Shubrick*, his leave-taking was far from normal.

After a short, unsuccessful trip north to the Fraser River country in British Columbia where the gold fever was intense, Henry George returned to San Francisco at the end of November "dead broke." Soon, however, he went to work setting type. Several months later, when business fell off in the firm for which he was working, he lost his job and went to Sacramento, picking up odd jobs here and there. Once again back in San Francisco, David Bond, who had secured the typesetting job for George in December, got him another on the *California Home Journal*. The job brought George into contact with literature once again; and as in the winter that had just passed when Henry was living at the "What Cheer House" where he had access to a rather good collection of books, he was able to read widely and intensively. During this period he first gave his wholehearted attention to Adam Smith's *Wealth of Nations*, a book that was to figure continually in George's intellectual interests. Through 1860, George worked as an apprentice printer in anticipation of his twenty-first birthday in September, for then he would be able to claim the earnings of a journeyman and double his twelve-dollar salary. During the next year or two, he had at least six different printing jobs, finally arriving as an embryo newspaperman. However, the years 1860-61 were marked by two important events, one national and the other personal: South Carolina seceded from the Union, precipitating the Civil War; Henry George and Annie Corsina Fox eloped and were married.

In 1861, amidst war and marriage, George invested one hundred dollars in partnership with several others to buy the San Francisco *Daily Evening Journal*. "He pushed," Barker remarks, "for a policy of literary-interest and human-interest journalism, like that to which he was accustomed on the *Home Journal*."[7] By summer, George was very optimistic about the paper's future; circulation was about three thousand. However, by early fall the newspaper was on the verge of collapse and the partnership nearing dissolution. The war was already in progress when George, three months before his marriage, wrote his sister Jennie about his thoughts and beliefs now that he had just passed his twenty-second birthday.

This long "millennial" letter of September 15th describes more accurately than any other document the state of Henry George's mind at this critical juncture in his personal fortunes. It was "a season of sorrows . . . Yet," as Barker writes, "the letter is engaging because [George] wrote into it a connected estimate of his roles in life, as citizen, son, and Christian, and as a man of personal ambition."[8] George's comments about the paper's destiny are clear: "I have felt unsettled and worried about business —hoping that each day would make some change, that I might tell you of. In fact, until a few days past, hardly knowing whether our paper would get through the next day, as I feared something would occur to bring it to a close—and, in truth, feeling something like the sailor in a calm, when wishing for even —'Storm or hurricane,/Anything, to put a close/To this most dread, monotonous repose.'"

It is interesting to note George's affinity for the sea image. He was surely having trouble reconciling his and America's dream of the millennium with the current facts of existence. As he goes on to say, "what a constant reaching this life is, a constant stretching forth, and longing after something. But you know what Emerson in the 'Sphinx' makes his 'Oedipus' say:

> 'The fiend that man harries
> Is love of the best—
> Yawns the pit of the dragon
> Lit by the rays from the blest.'"

After the sea image, he turns to Emerson, and then he continues: "And so it is—and so it will be until we reach the perfect, and that, you and I, and every son of Adam and every daughter of Eve, each for himself, knows we are very far from." This spiritual yearning is everywhere present in *Progress and Poverty*. George often wonders how man and how America is to secure the happiness they pursue, when life and liberty are not the concrete realities that self-evident truths should be. "Our country is being torn to pieces, and ourselves [,] our homes, filled with distress. As to the ultimate end I have no doubt; if civil war should pass over the whole country, leaving nothing but devastation behind it, I think my faith in the ultimate good would remain unchanged, but it is hard to feel so of our individual cases—On great events and movements we can philosophize, but when it comes down to ourselves, to those we love, then we can only feel—our philosophy goes to the dogs. . . ."

The entire letter expresses the alternate nay-saying and yea-saying of nineteenth-century British and American writing, reminding the reader of the mingled doubt and belief that is evident in Carlyle, Emerson, Melville, and Whitman. George's dream, which has so much in common with Thoreau's and with America's, is best characterized by his own observations upon his personal and philosophic perspectives. "How I long for the Golden Age—for the promised Millenium [sic], when each one will be free to follow his best and noblest impulses, unfettered by the restrictions and necessities which our present state of society imposes upon him—when the poorest and the meanest will have a chance to use all his God-given faculties, and not be forced to drudge away the best part of his time in order to supply wants but little above those of the animal."[9] By November the partnership in the *Journal* dissolved, and George entered upon a hectic courtship and runaway marriage in the worst of financial straits. For several years George was in many ways "forced to drudge away . . . in order to supply wants but little above those of the animal."

Annie Fox, who had been reared as a Roman Catholic, and Henry George were married in a Methodist Church whose broad-minded minister read the marriage service of the Episcopal Church in which Henry had been reared because it "more nearly approached the Catholic." George had shortly before joined the Methodist Church not so much from religious convictions as from fellowship with ardent Methodists who were his friends and shared his hopes for a better society.

The elopement unfortunately cut off Annie Fox from her family. Lodging in various places in both San Francisco and Sacramento, the war years passed slowly for the Georges. In the fall of 1862, Henry George, Jr. was born. The recent sorrow at the loss of his sister was thus eased some by the birth of his son. George's first biographer, Henry George, Jr., gives us a good account, although secondhand, of his father's reaction to his sister Jennie's death:

> . . . springing to his feet and pacing the floor, as was his habit when mentally roused, [George] protested that he could not bring himself to believe that his dear sister was dead; and with the manner of sudden conviction, said that there *must* be, there *is*, another life—that the soul *is* immortal. But his words expressed his longing, rather than his conviction. Immortality he now earn-

estly wished to believe in. But the theology of his youth did not persuade him, and it was not until many years afterwards when pursuing the great inquiry that produced "Progress and Poverty" that he perceived the "grand simplicity and unspeakable harmony of universal law," that beneficence and intelligence govern social laws, instead of blind, clashing forces; and then faith from reason came and immortality became a fixed belief.[10]

The statement on immortality which concludes *Progress and Poverty* is eloquent testimony to the conviction that actually did characterize Henry George's intellectual maturity. The appeal which *Progress and Poverty* had for many people can be traced in part to its transcendental expressions of religious belief as much as to its economic pragmatism.

IV *Burning Issues and the Beginnings of a Newspaper Career*

In 1863, in the midst of the Civil War, two more events figured in the life of the young Henry George: President Lincoln issued his Emancipation Proclamation and Leland Stanford, the president of the Central Pacific Railroad Company, became the Republican Governor of the State of California. As a fellow Republican, George shared the national views of the party; but his ideas and those of Stanford, whatever personal admiration George had for Stanford as a fellow townsman, were inevitably to clash. Several years later when George's views were beginning to crystallize, his opposition to the new western railroad barons was expressed in part in one of his first extended essays, "What the Railroad Will Bring Us" (1868). In 1863, however, Henry George was still struggling to create a system of his own and to live by it. The diary he kept during these years of personal privation records his decision for a career as a writer. By the spring of 1865, he writes, "Concluded that the best I could do would be to go home and write a little. Came home and wrote for the sake of practice an essay on the 'Use of Time,' which occupied me until Annie prepared dinner."[11] He was in actuality still a printer, and jobs came and went as he moved from paper to paper in Sacramento and in San Francisco.

George often went through the kind of mental torture which the self-educated man often inflicts upon himself. Writing about

"Time" made him realize how much of his twenty-five years had been spent uselessly. His regret reflects the standards of an age different from today's; for, though George was still to see his way, he had stored up experiences that were to make it possible for him, like Melville,[12] to date his life from his twenty-fifth year. He was unimpressed by the fact that his experiences were in some ways more valuable than a formal education, no matter how much he may have felt the absence of the latter. He decided to "endeavour to acquire facility and elegance in the expression of [his] thoughts by writing essays or other matters which [he] will preserve for future comparison. And in this practice it will be well," he concluded, "to aim at mechanical neatness and grace, as well as at proper and polished language."[13]

Interestingly enough, George turned to writing about the problem of labor; and in correspondence with the *Journal of the Trades and Workmen* he wrote on the printers' union and maritime labor. Soon after his "article about laws relating to sailors," George published a "Plea for the Supernatural" in the *Californian* which was also publishing the work of other young writers, including Mark Twain and Bret Harte. George drew on his sailing experiences aboard the *Hindoo* and the *Shubrick*. The "Plea for the Supernatural" was even republished in the Boston Saturday *Evening Gazette*. And though George's biographers are correct in not taking this essay as a "literal confession of belief,"[14] it is nevertheless interesting to note that the pragmatic and the supernatural were ever present in George's mental make-up. And it is worth remembering that his masterwork, *Progress and Poverty*, is both pragmatic and idealistic, economic and religious, hard-headed and transcendental. For George, the natural and the supernatural were equal parts of the human continuum.

Within a month of the appearance of George's articles in the California magazines of early spring 1865, the Civil War came to an end. On the morning of April 15, 1865, news reached San Francisco that President Lincoln had been assassinated. Amid the riotous turmoil and shocked sorrow, George wrote a lengthy letter to the *Alta California*. Tempted to take part with some of his friends who were vengefully destroying the type and offices of pro-southern newspapers, his frustration at not being able to exercise his passions by physical means forced him to his pen. The letter "Sic Semper Tyrannis!" was printed in a special increased opportunities; those who have only their own labour will become poorer, and find it harder to get ahead—first because it will take more capital to buy land or to get into business, and second, because as competition reduces the wages of labour, this capital will be harder for them to obtain.

. . . let us not forget that the character of a people counts for more than their numbers; that the distribution of wealth is even a more important matter than its production. Let us not imagine ourselves in a fool's paradise, where the golden apples will drop into our mouths; let us not think that after the stormy seas and head gales of all the ages, *our* ship has at last struck the trade winds of time. The future of our State, of our nation, of our race, looks fair and bright; perhaps the future looked so to the philosophers who once sat in the porches of Athens—to the unremembered men who raised the cities whose ruins lie south of us. Our modern civilization strikes broad and deep and looks high. So did the tower which men once built almost unto heaven.[17]

Henry George's style is already marked: the sea metaphor with the effective pun upon "trade," the sense of history, the emphasis upon character and ethics, and the biblical allusion. Henry George very early sided with labor and sought an increased distribution of wealth. His description of what the railroad would bring, besides its obvious benefits, shows us the soil from which were to grow the vines that were to produce, in turn, the grapes of wrath of the later California of John Steinbeck. The end of the year 1868 brought new challenges and a decade of thought and experience, all of which went into the making of *Progress and Poverty*.

The Search for a Meaningful Role

edition of the *Alta California* on April 16th. A eulogy of Lincoln, the piece captured the irony of the death in April—"What fitting time! Good Friday! . . ." George proclaimed: "While the world lasts will this scene be remembered. As a martyr of freedom—as the representative of the justice of a great nation, the name of the victim will live forever; and the Proclamation of Emancipation, signed with the name and sealed with the blood of *Abraham Lincoln* will remain a land mark in the progress of the race." He pressed the irony of Booth's alleged words, "*Sic semper tyrannis*: the South is avenged!"

A week or so later, George wrote another letter, more sober and restrained, which was simply entitled *Abraham Lincoln* and which appeared as a front-page editorial in the *Alta California's* regular Sunday edition. Once again George returned to the theme of democratic idealism, "No other system would have produced him [Lincoln]; through no crowd of courtiers could such a man have forced his way. . . . And, as in our time of need, the man that was needed came forth, let us know that it will always be so, and that under our institutions, when the rights of the people are endangered, from their ranks will spring the men for the times." Lincoln was "no common man, yet the qualities which made him great were eminently common."

George's first letter led to his being offered his first full-fledged reportorial job. Besides his assignment to describe the mourning for Lincoln in the city, the *Alta California* also asked him to send back dispatches from Mexico where George was planning to go in what proved to be an abortive expedition in support of Juarez. In some ways George never gave up his romantic revolutionary principles—a state of mind characteristically American. The underdog always won George's sympathies if his cause was just. Soon after the failure of the expedition—the ship was halted by the Coast Guard—George joined the Monroe League, a short-lived organization which supported the point of view of the Monroe Doctrine and republican freedom for Mexico.

Like Milton or any modern supporter of war crimes trials, George later, as a responsible newspaper editor, defended the execution of Maximilian. His voice, that of English liberty and Protestant democracy, was justifying the right of the people to depose its leader, whether king or president. On July 3, 1867, in a San Francisco *Times* editorial, George wrote that the execution of Maximilian was "a protest against the right of Kings to cause suffering and shed blood for their own selfish ends. . . . It will teach princes and princelings to be more cautious how they endeavour to subvert the liberties of a free people."

Through the next year, much of it spent in Sacramento, George wrote a number of essays, some of which appeared in the Sacramento *Union*. After using his sea experiences for a few more pieces on the supernatural, he turned his attention to labor questions, writing under the apt pen name "Proletarian." His articles were well received, but it was essentially free-lance work. With a wife and three children to support, a steady income was a necessity. In November, 1866, the opportunity finally came: George joined the newly organized San Francisco *Times*. By the next June, he was managing editor. He remained in this position for about fourteen months, and this tenure as an editor marked his first extended experience at what was to be, generally speaking, his life's work.

Of the *Times* period as a preparation for things to come, his son writes that it "related to style in writing and development in thinking. While his style always had been free and natural, he had from the beginning aimed at compactness, and it was to the necessity of re-writing news articles and compressing them into condensed items . . ."[15] that proved lastingly invaluable. Besides affecting his style, George's first editorial experiences forced him to examine in detail the social and economic problems of California, including labor supply and wages, land settlement and land policy. Barker sees the later Henry George in one of the *Times* editorials:

> "The interests of the State are the interests of its citizens—the greater the rewards which labor receives, the higher the estimation in which it is held, the greater the equality of the distribution of earnings and property, the more virtuous, intelligent and independent are the masses of the people, the stronger, richer, and nobler is the state. Free trade, labor-saving machinery, cooperative organizations, will enable us to produce more cheaply, and with a positive increase of wages; but it would be better for California that she should retain only her present sparse but independent and comfortable population, than that she should have all of England's wealth and millions with all of her destitution

and pauperism." It would be interesting to know what writers or books George had in mind as the sources of his "fundamental principles of political economy." [Mentioned earlier in this editorial debate with the *Alta California*.] Perhaps he had drawn on some ideas of Wells or had been influenced by Henry Carey. His editorial reads more like the 1930s than the 1860s, and more like Henry George's future books than like the British treatises on economics which might have come most readily to hand for reference.[16]

George was clearly in the process of working his way back to Jacksonian principles and to the party of his father, as well as looking into the future. Once slavery had been "abolished" and Lincoln was no more, George saw that the Republican Party and policy was to become the enemy of the reform he sought. Like the *Times* itself, however, George was still officially Republican, but *he* was also a radical. Both he and the paper voiced concern that private speculation was destroying American freedom and that the loss of free or public lands for public use would eventually mean the end of political and economic liberty, and the end of equality.

When George left the *Times* in August, 1868, the railroad question was receiving editorial attention. In October, George published a seven-thousand-word article in the *Overland Monthly* entitled "What the Railroad Will Bring Us." It was the lead article in the *Overland*'s fourth issue; Noah Brooks was one of the journal's assistant editors, and among its contributors were Mark Twain, Bret Harte, and Joaquin Miller.

"What the Railroad Will Bring Us" summarizes George's political and economic views before he headed east in the employ of the San Francisco *Herald* to do battle with monopoly for the first time. George wrote not only in his usual prophetic style, but he sounded a warning which has since proven to have been justified:

> The truth is, that the completion of the railroad and the consequent great increase of business and population, will not be a benefit to all of us, but only to a portion. As a general rule (liable of course to exceptions) those who have, it will make wealthier; for those who have not, it will make it more difficult to get. Those who have lands, mines, established businesses, special abilities of certain kind, will become richer for it and find

increased opportunities; those who have only their own labour will become poorer, and find it harder to get ahead—first because it will take more capital to buy land or to get into business, and second, because as competition reduces the wages of labour, this capital will be harder for them to obtain.

. . . let us not forget that the character of a people counts for more than their numbers; that the distribution of wealth is even a more important matter than its production. Let us not imagine ourselves in a fool's paradise, where the golden apples will drop into our mouths; let us not think that after the stormy seas and head gales of all the ages, *our* ship has at last struck the trade winds of time. The future of our State, of our nation, of our race, looks fair and bright; perhaps the future looked so to the philosophers who once sat in the porches of Athens—to the unremembered men who raised the cities whose ruins lie south of us. Our modern civilization strikes broad and deep and looks high. So did the tower which men once built almost unto heaven.[17]

Henry George's style is already marked: the sea metaphor with the effective pun upon "trade," the sense of history, the emphasis upon character and ethics, and the biblical allusion. Henry George very early sided with labor and sought an increased distribution of wealth. His description of what the railroad would bring, besides its obvious benefits, shows us the soil from which were to grow the vines that were to produce, in turn, the grapes of wrath of the later California of John Steinbeck. The end of the year 1868 brought new challenges and a decade of thought and experience, all of which went into the making of *Progress and Poverty*.

CHAPTER 2

A Prophet in the Making:
Writings before *Progress and Poverty*

I *The Fight Against Monopoly*

DURING the late summer and fall of 1868, a week after he
quit the *Times*, George became managing editor of the
San Francisco *Chronicle*. Two weeks after he began work at his
new job, he sent his family to Philadelphia. Before he joined
them, he was busy at the *Chronicle*, establishing what was to be
in broad terms the permanent point of view of the *Chronicle's*
editorial policy. He attacked land speculation, monopoly in landholding, and the supporters of cheap labor. But George was too
aggressive, and he could not get on with Charles de Young, the
Chronicle's owner. Though George's effect on the *Chronicle* was
lasting and important, he did not remain managing editor long
enough to see out the fall in the newspaper's employ.

The chance to go east came when John Nugent decided to re-
establish his San Francisco *Herald*. He asked George to go to
New York on behalf of the *Herald* to request permission to join
the Associated Press. As an alternate plan should the *Herald* be
refused its request, Nugent suggested that George organize a
special news service for the San Francisco paper. At the beginning of December, George headed east by the overland route,
taking the stage which connected the Central Pacific and the
Union Pacific—the transcontinental railroad still short of com-
pletion. From his personal experience as an average traveler, he
concluded that the railroad, despite its public subsidies and land
grants, had not lowered the expense of coast-to-coast travel and
that its roadbeds were particularly engineered with an eye for
higher government subsidies. He considered Wells Fargo dis-
gracefully incompetent in its handling of the United States mails.

As far as George was concerned, the results of monopoly were as obvious as they were inevitable.

While George was in the East, Nugent (in January) began publication of the *Herald*, even though it was barred—as was the *Chronicle* and several other California papers—from the California Press Association that alone had access to the Associated Press news service and its coast-to-coast wire. George could get nowhere with the Association, but he did manage to get an informal offer from Western Union in New York City for five hundred words a day at five hundred dollars a month. With the help of his boyhood friend John Hasson, George arranged with the Harrisburg (Pennsylvania) *Patriot and Union* to have its Associated Press news dispatches as soon as they were received. The dispatches were then sent from Harrisburg to Philadelphia where they were put on the Western Union wire to San Francisco. George's system of circumventing the press associations made it possible for Nugent to begin the publication of the *Herald* by announcing to its readers its access to transcontinental telegraphic news despite the monopoly of the state press association.

George understood the close relation of Western Union and the Associated Press, but he still hoped the telegraph company would continue to honor its oral agreement with him. After several months of harassing George, Western Union in April, 1869, finally refused to permit George the use of its services. It offered him a new contract at a 122 per cent increase which the *Herald*, of course, could not afford. The press monopoly had won, and George was disappointed and angry. He felt that the Associated Press-Western Union combine had arrogantly defied the rights of all to the access of news. A month or so earlier (March 5th), George had written a signed letter to the New York *Tribune* that had attacked the Central Pacific Railroad for its excessive charges and political power, as well as Wells Fargo for its reckless handling of the mails. Now, in late April, he wrote again to attack in public the monopoly in communications which he felt equaled that in transportation and public service—a more dangerously undemocratic monopoly. Only the New York *Herald*, among major newspapers, published George's protest against the Associated Press monopoly. Though the New York *Herald* ran the story in its Sunday edition of April 25th and commented favorably in an editorial, George saw that no other major newspaper even touched the story. So far as he was concerned, the San Francisco *Herald* was a victim of a big business operation that had wounded the freedom of the press and made a financial killing in the bargain.

Before heading back to San Francisco, George's hand-to-hand combat with monopoly led him into the curious position of opposing Chinese immigration, a keen issue on the West Coast. Of course, his stand was part of his continual opposition to wage slavery. Just days prior to departure, he submitted an article to the New York *Tribune*, whose managing editor was his friend John Russell Young, and whose editor-in-chief was Horace Greeley, whom George several years later supported for the presidency against a second term for President Grant. The *Tribune* of May 1, 1869, carried George's article "The Chinese on the Pacific Coast" along with the first installment of Greeley's essays on political economy. George's letter "was to influence his coming California career rather more as a student and editor and social critic than as a young man interested in practical politics."[1] On leaving New York, George ironically observed: "I am doing well for a young man . . . I have already got the Central Pacific, Wells Fargo, and Western Union down on me, and it will be just my luck to offend the Bank of California next."[2]

Though he used almost any religious or racial argument to sway his readers, George's essential complaint against Chinese immigration stemmed from his conflict with the railroad. Chinese labor was coolie labor: "Plainly, when we speak of a reduction of wages in any general and permanent sense, we mean this, if we mean anything—that in the division of the joint production of labour and capital, the share of labor is to be smaller, that of capital larger. This is precisely what the reduction of wages consequent upon the introduction of Chinese labor means."[3]

In a speech in San Francisco some twenty years later (February, 1890), George recalled having asked an old gold miner in 1858 what harm the Chinese had done him:

> "No harm now; but it will not be always that wages are as high as they are to-day in California. As the country grows, as people come in, wages will go down, and some day or other white men will be glad to get these diggings that the Chinamen are now

working." And I well remember how it impressed me, the idea that as the country grew in all that we are hoping that it might grow, the condition of those who had to work for their living must grow, not better, but worse.[4]

More than ten years before his letter to the *Tribune*, George had been confronted with the problem that was to be the basis of *Progress and Poverty*.

He broke now with Nugent and the doomed San Francisco *Herald* (Nugent had tried to avoid paying George seven hundred dollars in back wages). At loose ends because he was not to be the western correspondent of the New York *Tribune*, though he had been so contracted, George turned briefly once again to typesetting. His family was still in the East; and Young, no longer with the *Tribune*, could do nothing about preventing the paper from canceling George's contract with them. In between causes, George found himself substituting for an ill friend as acting editor of the San Francisco *Monitor*, a local Catholic weekly. It was not long before land monopoly questions arose and the editorials became more and more Georgian. He kept slipping Irish grievances into the paper and even attacked the San Francisco *Bulletin* for its "Hanglo-Saxon" point of view, a strong indication, also, that in opposing Chinese immigration he was not interested primarily in jingoistic or racial questions but in economic problems and poverty amidst progress.

On a recommendation of California's incumbent liberal Democratic Governor, Henry H. Haight, with whom George had become acquainted, he became editor in September, 1869, of the Oakland *Daily Transcript*. He immediately renewed his attack upon monopolistic enterprises and parties. In editorial after editorial, George criticized the land monopolists and the railroads, taking care as always to indicate the worth of the railroad in and for itself. By spring, 1870, George had outgrown his job on the *Transcript*, and Governor Haight invited him to take over the editorship of the Democratic party's major paper, the Sacramento *Reporter*, known in earlier years as the *State Capital Reporter*.

Governor Haight's political plans grew. He decided to try to curb the power of the Central Pacific through anti-monopolistic legislation for which he sought popular support. With Haight's blessing, George attacked the railroad's subsidy policy and its monopolistic practices. Henry George, Jr., briefly describes the enemy as his father and Governor Haight had seen it:

> . . . a monster of fairy lore, . . . gulping down lands, bonds and money showered upon it, all the while like a weakling pleading for more. The plain and palpable fact was that leaving out of consideration the imperial endowment in lands, it had already received several times more money, or what could immediately be turned into money, than was necessary to build the system, and that contemporary with the work of railroad construction had arisen the private fortunes of the big four manipulating the corporation—Stanford, Crocker, Huntington and Hopkins, who, from comparative poverty, had quickly risen to the class of multi-millionaires.[5]

Almost immediately after George took over at the *Reporter*, a press war began. He was involved again with Western Union and the Associated Press, for the new war was in reality little more than a resumption of old hostilities. But this time George gained the victory he had longed for a year before. The rival telegraph company that George predicted would challenge Western Union came into the communications field. The new company, the Atlantic and Pacific, and the American Press Association, with George's old friend Hasson as "general agent," broke the transcontinental monopoly of wire and news. Since the American Press Association had John Russell Young as its president, it came as no surprise that George was made the new press association's California agent. California papers, including De Young's San Francisco *Chronicle*, having been shut out by the Associated Press, had no choice but to join the American Press Association.

In editorials, George happily hailed the new free trade in news, and he reacted ironically to the plight of the California Associated Press papers that were now forced to cut their prices. For so long as he was editor of the *Reporter*, George kept the heat on the Associated Press and also on the railroads. George was beginning to make the point he was to make over and over again in the years to come: public transport and public communication should not be in the control of private corporations. It was essentially an argument for nationalization by necessity. Corporate monopolies had to be regulated for the public good by the government acting on behalf of the people as a whole.

George's pen had become a force to be reckoned with in California; and the Central Pacific, whose overwhelming influence in California was incalculable, struck back. After failing to tempt George by winning him over to its side or to insure his silence in the future, the Central Pacific arranged for a "neutral" party to buy the *Reporter*. Before Governor Haight's warning against a fast deal reached Sacramento (the governor was away from the capital at the time), the paper had been purchased by the "neutral" party with Central Pacific money. George was out, and from that moment the Sacramento *Reporter* became "the obsequious organ of the Railroad Company." In the year to come, the railroad corporation was to throw its full weight into the election in order to defeat Governor Haight, the entire Democratic party, and the subsidy policies with which George and Governor Haight were associated.

Monopoly, though temporarily stymied, had won again. George had only the satsifaction of losing on principle. He had helped to break the news monopoly, and he had had his say in editorials and in two long pamphlets, *The Subsidy Question and the Democratic Party* and *Our Land and Land Policy*. As a former supporter of Lincoln, he was well on his way to defending the philosophy of the Declaration of Independence and the "Republicanism of Jefferson and the Democracy of Jackson," which he was soon to declare broadly to be his fundamental point of view. In later years, he could look back to the vision he had had in New York City in the midst of his first large-scale struggle with monopoly as the beginning of his unswerving dedication to reform.

II *Visions, Illuminations, and John Stuart Mill*

During the years in which Henry George first began his lifelong quarrel with vested interests, he had several insights into the problems that he felt beset society. One memorable occasion was his attempt to circumvent the Associated Press-Western Union combine as Eastern representative of the San Francisco *Herald*. In a letter dated February 1, 1883, to Father Thomas Dawson of Glencree, Ireland, he recalled the spirit that had moved him: "Because you are not only my friend, but a priest and a religious I will say something that I don't like to speak of—that I never before have told any one. Once, in daylight, and in a city street there came to me a thought, a vision, a call— give it what name you please. But every nerve quivered. And there and then I made a vow. Through evil and through good, whatever I have done and whatever I have left undone, to that I have been true."[6]

In his acceptance speech for his first New York City mayoralty nomination in 1886, he described what it was that made him pledge himself with such transcendental fervor to the reformation of society: "Years ago I came to this city from the West, unknown, knowing nobody, and I saw and recognized for the first time the shocking contrast between monstrous wealth and debasing want. And here I made a vow, from which I have never faltered, to seek out and remedy, if I could, the cause that condemned little children to lead such a life as you know them to lead in the squalid districts."[7]

The reality of his New York vision and the loyalty he felt for his vow were given added impetus by his so-called Oakland "illumination." While editor of the Oakland *Daily Transcript*, George was riding one day in the foothills outside the town when he came through a casual meeting to understand vividly and concretely "the reason of advancing poverty with advancing wealth":

> Absorbed in my own thoughts, I had driven the horse into the hills until he panted. Stopping for breath, I asked a passing teamster, for want of something better to say, what land was worth there. He pointed to some cows grazing off so far that they looked like mice and said: "I don't know exactly, but there is a man over there who will sell some land for a thousand dollars an acre." Like a flash it came upon me that there was the reason of advancing poverty with advancing wealth. With the growth of population, land grows in value, and the men who work it must pay more for the privilege. I turned back, amidst quiet thought, to the perception that then came to me and has been with me ever since.[8]

Of course, those who gained control of the land early and could patiently wait made great profits with no exertion. When land passed into private hands, all improvement in the area in question went to enriching the landowner and not to the people who worked it or to the nation and the public to whom it truly belonged.

George's reading and correspondence with John Stuart Mill added the intellectual force necessary to sustain and formalize his own insights and mystical experiences, thereby strengthening his personal opinions about current social, political, and economic problems. His initial connection with Mill arose from his letter to the New York *Tribune* on Chinese immigration. Though he was one day soon, as editor of the San Francisco *Post*, to express some reservations about Mill, he read Mill's *Principles of Political Economy* in 1869 for what was apparently the first time. At least there is no evidence that he had read Mill any earlier than his stay in Philadelphia when he came east to arrange for transcontinental news dispatches to be sent to the San Francisco *Herald*. His argument against the immigration of coolie labor is based upon the wages-fund theory for which he was partially in debt to Mill. Chinese labor, he reasoned, would bring down wages and reduce trade not only in California but all across the country. Wage rates were determined in most cases by the size of the labor force, and any indiscriminate importation of what was a kind of slave labor would affect the nation's economy disastrously. Though he makes references to racial, moral, and religious differences between the Chinese and other people on the West Coast, the major and intellectual force of his argument is based upon economic principles. George clipped his letter to the *Tribune* from the paper and, after reaching California in the late spring, sent it to Mill. After all, since he had based his argument largely upon Mill's views, he felt it would be interesting to see what the master's reaction would be.

At an opportune time months later (November, 1869), George, then editor of the *Transcript*, received Mill's reply. In the November 20th issue of the paper, he published a long editorial and printed Mill's letter in full. After quoting Mill's recommendations, George concluded that Mill's opinion "entirely" justified his own. Mill had written that "Concerning the purely economic view . . . I entirely agree with you; and it could be hardly better stated and argued than it is in your able article in the New York Tribune. That the Chinese immigration, if it attains great dimensions, must be economically injurious to the mass of the present population; that it must diminish their wages, and reduce them to a lower stage of physical comfort and well-being, I have no manner of doubt. Nothing can be more fallacious than the attempts to make out that thus to lower wages is the way to raise them. . . ." Mill did not miss touching upon the question of out and out slavery which was, indeed, involved in the importation of the Chinese: "One kind of restrictive measure seems to me not only desirable, but absolutely called for; the most stringent laws against introducing Chinese immigrants as Coolies, i.e. under contracts binding them to the service of particular persons. All such obligations are a form of compulsory labour, that is, of slavery. . . ."[9]

Needless to say, George made a great splash with the Mill letter. It was the first time he became truly notorious in his "home" city as a spokesman for a cause. His *Transcript* days that had begun suspiciously led, therefore, to his prominence as the editor of the Sacramento *Reporter* the next year. Indeed, the Mill business was harangued for months afterwards. After the initial reactions of pro-Chinese and anti-Chinese immigration newspapers in San Francisco, which only served to spread the fame of the *Transcript* and its editor, the Chicago *Tribune* commented editorially upon the controversy by citing a letter from Mill to Horace White, the editor, which said Mill's letter must have been inaccurately quoted by George. Of course, White published Mill's statement.

By this time George was already editor of the *Reporter*; and with the Chicago *Tribune* attacking him at long distance and with the San Francisco *Bulletin* sneering at him for purposely garbling Mill's original letter, he had ample reason to reprint the entire correspondence. He then sent the complete series of newspaper items to Mill, who with graceful kindness and absolute honesty, but without any further discussion, acknowledged that George had in fact reproduced his letter accurately and fully. The controversy over his reliability and honesty as a journalist had enabled George to restate his ideas and to make political hay out of it all in the midst of the Democratic campaign in California.

That George was grateful to Mill for ideas, as well as for courtesies, can be seen both in the tribute he paid Mill at the end of his editorial in November, 1869, and in the letter he wrote to him the next summer (July 16, 1870), some six months after his Oakland "illumination": "In an endeavour to account for the continuance of pauperism in England, and the gradual sinking of the working-classes in the older parts of the states, I have come to conclusions which were cleared and strengthened by your works. . . ." In the early 1870's, as *Our Land and Land Policy* was to prove, George was beginning to organize his economic views.

III   *George's Editorial Opinions and the San Francisco Post*

From 1869 to 1875, George's newspaper career in San Francisco was a hectic but a fruitful one. During this interval many of his fundamental ideas and perspectives were completely formed and clearly expressed. Though he certainly had not found as yet a definite scheme or system for his thoughts on the scale of the one in *Progress and Poverty*, random editorials in the San Francisco *Monitor*, in the Oakland *Daily Transcript*, in the Sacramento *Reporter*, and finally, more fully and frequently, in the San Francisco *Post* chart the development of his thinking. Coupled with his pamphlet *Our Land and Land Policy* in 1871, and his speeches in the late 1870's, yet to be discussed, his newspaper editorials consistently led him to the conclusions and to the style that found full expression in all his later work.

In several of his editorials in the *Monitor* in 1869, George attacked the land problems of Ireland, a subject with which he was to be very closely associated in the 1880's; his comments foreshadowed much that was to come. In the *Monitor* of September 11, he wrote: "beneath the Irish land question is the English land question. . . . What is there in the laws of entail and primogeniture that should set aside the God-given law, that these who toil shall enjoy the fruits of the earth?" On problems in California he said the state had reached a point of decision from which there would be no return. It could either go the way of the rest of the world, ridden to death by armies of capitalists and land speculators, or force the big land aggregators to bear the burden through "full taxation." He proposed graduated taxation so that larger estates would be made to pay higher taxes than smaller ones. George wanted to break the hold of the monopolizers so that public land would be protected from private absorption before the vast tracts of California and of the West were completely lost and the many natural resources captured by those engaged in building personal fortunes at public expense.

Later in the same year, while editor of the *Transcript*, George continued his probing of economic and political questions, especially those which interested him most—free trade and monopoly. His views were consistent in general with both his past and his future opinions: he was against protection of private interests. It was in the *Transcript* that, in order to support labor and encourage immigration from the eastern states, George had published the letter he had received from Mill supporting his stand on Chinese immigration. It had divided the press on the West Coast and had clearly placed George in the camp of the Democratic and Jeffersonian agrarians. During his tenure as editor of the *Transcript*, George consolidated his ideas about speculation and the national banking policy, both of which he opposed. But his notoriety as Mill's correspondent and as an opponent of Chinese immigration was the most prominent feature of the *Transcript* days. The papers who opposed George called him a demogogue and a "vulgar, self-advertising showman." Others felt he was not only correct but had seriously undertaken to examine a nasty problem with candor and honesty. As Barker has observed, George, as of March, 1869, "had essayed the burden of asserting nationality while denying monopoly—surely as awkward a burden as a democratic theorist has ever undertaken."[10]

As editor of the Sacramento *Reporter*, George's political and economic thought not only continued to mature but also started to formalize. He took what could be described as a recognizable *contemporary* political stance. Two major issues governed his experiences on the *Reporter*—state control of monopolies and taxation. Having sided with an old-line Democrat like Governor Haight, George had not only attacked the subsidies given the railroads but had also aligned himself with the Democratic party's unsuccessful effort to maintain and to increase its power in the state. The positions he took were familiar to him and were as much an outgrowth of his father's political associations as they were an inevitable development of his own ideas. These positions are best indicated in "What the Railroad Will Bring Us."

Without Lincoln and the struggle to end human bondage, the Republican party and he had little in common. As editor of the *Reporter*, he was given the opportunity of attacking the unfair taxation of small property holders and of existence or subsistence farmers. He was led to the point of pleading for the nationalization of at least one giant monopoly while preaching steadily in his editorials that the "great NEED of California" was "free trade."

George, in his desire for social revolution, went so far as to support the international labor movement then gathering force in Europe, but at that time he knew little of the radical socialism with which it was imbued and which in later years he could never bring himself to trust. Always a political maverick, he opposed Governor Haight and the state's Democratic organization on several occasions because he wanted them to resemble him rather than make himself over to reflect them. On no point was he more clear about his point of view than on the question of the ratification of the Fifteenth Amendment to the Constitution. George felt that the Democrats of California were not giving the amendment their wholehearted support and he said so. For George, monopoly was wrong on any scale. Therefore, *because*, more than *despite*, his opinions on Chinese immigration, which stemmed from his belief that the Chinese were being used by organized capital to depress wages, George could not accept in any way the logic or morality of those who opposed equal rights for white and non-white citizens. For George, the Civil War was unfinished, and it was the duty of the Democratic party, in his eyes, to take the lead in reform, despite its latent racism and its opposition to Lincoln. Long a supporter of the eight-hour day, wage slavery was to George merely another form of human bondage; and he felt that the Democratic party was more given to listening to the pleas of the wage earner than was Grant's party. This position is that which many political liberals have taken in the hundred years of American history that have elapsed since George's struggles for social reform in the decade after the Civil War.

George's longest and most important association with a newspaper in the 1860's and 70's was with the San Francisco *Daily Evening Post*. He finally had the opportunity to create a paper of his own. With two partners, the printer W. M. Hinton, who admired *Our Land and Land Policy*, and A. H. Rapp, George began publishing the *Post* on December 4, 1871. In order to survive, of course, the paper had to make money. It was, therefore, a typical California newspaper and not at all like George's New York weekly of fifteen years later, *The Standard*, a reform movement journal. In what would be called today an advertising "gimmick," the *Post* introduced the copper penny to San Francisco on a large scale as part of an opening campaign to get readers. The partners had persuaded the Bank of California to release one thousand dollars in pennies to advertise the first newspaper to sell for one cent west of the Rockies.

From the beginning, the prime object of the paper was to interest the workingman—the Henry George man. George wanted the policies of the *Post* to form and to organize the thoughts and opinions—the aspirations—of the wage earner on the West Coast. In his first editorial, which was to give the paper its direction, he announced that the "Great Work of Reform" requires "a union of the good men of both parties," "economy in government," a reduction in taxes, a reformed civil service system, and a decentralization of power and wealth, including a de-emphasis upon the nation's tendency to encourage the growth of business and landholding monopolies. The paper enthusiastically supported Horace Greeley against Grant and mourned his "utter" defeat in the 1872 election. Unbridled capitalism, led by Grant's cavalry, seemed to George to be overwhelming all the Jeffersonian and Jacksonian principles to which he was dedicated more intensely than ever.

From December, 1871, until November, 1875, the *Post* proclaimed the views of Henry George. Arguing against the San Francisco *Examiner* and proving with simple illustrations his contention that a land tax would help the farmer and not burden him as his opponents contended, George wrote "that to take the tax off of personal property and improvements, and to put it on the land, would leave the owners of land and improvements less to pay than they have now."[11] It would also force land speculators who were holding land in an unimproved condition to release it to those who would willingly put it into production. George was beginning to stress the single tax doctrine of his later years while reiterating in many of his *Post* editorials the views he had expressed in the *Reporter*. "If one would see where taxation is really felt, he must go to the people whom the tax-gatherer never visits; . . . where in heathen ignorance, little children are toiling out their lives amid the clatter of wheels and looms; to the slums and tenement rows, where the man from the new West cannot go without a sinking and sickening of the heart."[12] George argued that "the income from the land should support the Government, and not go to the enriching of one small class of the population."[13] He was elaborating and re-investigating the ideas he had presented in *Our Land and Land Policy*. Though the fundamentals of his attacks upon monopoly and land speculation had changed little, the structure of his argument became more complex and the import more intense and far-reaching; his comments on taxation in the *Post* were specifically detailed.

In the *Post*, also, George pressed his Jeffersonian theory of the "natural right" of men to the land and studied the relation of labor and capital to land or property; his attacks upon and investigations of theories of wages and population, which anticipated his discussions of the wages fund theory and the Malthusian doctrine in *Progress and Poverty*, reappear again and again in the *Post* editorials. He also expressed his belief that rent was a social product, that it was an economic evil when appropriated by private parties, and that taxation of labor was mistaken and unfair and discouraged incentive for social improvement.

One particular editorial from the *Post* (April 21, 1874), which he called "A Problem for Working Men," not only sums up his general editorial views expressed during the four years he was editor of the paper but also shows how the *Post* editorials are related to both *Our Land and Land Policy* and *Progress and Poverty*:

> Is it not universally true that as population grows and wealth increases the condition of the laboring classes becomes worse, and that the amount and depth of real poverty increases? . . . The explanation that as population increases there is a greater strain on natural resources, and that labor in the aggregate becomes less productive, does not suffice, for the economies of production and exchange . . . more than compensate for any greater strain on natural resources. . . . Why is it, then, . . . as population increases, and wealth increases, that the largest class of the com-

munity not only do not get any of the benefit, but become actually poorer?

. . . As population increases, land, and hardly anything else but land, becomes valuable. . . . Land ownership levies its tax upon all the productive classes.

What is the remedy?

To make land-owners bear the common burden—tax land and exempt everything else.

George's "New Declaration of Independence" was aimed at wage slavery. California was then, as it essentially still is, a state in which the landholdings were vast and the landholders powerful.

The *Post* had other interests than those of land agitation and related subjects. The attacks upon land monopoly were complemented by several liberal campaigns against other forms of injustice. Besides criticizing wide-open gambling, crime, corruption, and lynchings, the *Post* took the lead in publicizing the case of the ship *Sunrise*, which involved indefensible cruelty, and, at least, manslaughter. Like Cooper and Melville before him, George was a fierce opponent of maritime brutality and an outright spokesman for the common seaman. Because of his early experiences at sea, again like Cooper and Melville, he was well acquainted with the seaman's problems and with maritime management-labor difficulties and their relation to human rights.

The *Sunrise* case involved the deaths of three seamen who jumped from the ship and were drowned because of the cruelty of the captain and his first mate while the ship was en route from New York to San Francisco. The *Post* investigated and publicized the incident in spite of efforts made to suppress the entire matter. Demanding prosecution, George offered a reward for the apprehension of the captain and his mate after they had apparently disappeared from the scene. Hiring its own special counsel, the *Post* pursued the case until the captain was tried and convicted. The case closed as a newspaper story with an appeal for the foundation of a society for the protection of seamen. A seaman, in George's eyes, was a wage earner, not a slave; and he would not stand by without protest in order that unfair employment practices could continue. The case received national and international attention, and as in his battle with the Associated Press and Western Union, George had taken on the role of David.

This time, however, the judge of the people had won a clear victory.

George dreamed of the just state; and while the role of a David in San Francisco was important, it was in the role of a Moses that George was yet to be heard. His vision of the perfect state and his editorial judgments on social rights and wrongs led him inevitably to the problem of how laws could be framed so that the perfect state could come into being—a state in which the judgment of social inequities would become a needless activity. His July Fourth comments in 1874 incorporate his vision: "The great American Republic must be a republic in fact as well as form; a Christian republic in the full grand meaning of the words . . . till time shall come when warships, and standing armies, and paupers and prisons, and men toiling from sunrise to dusk, and women brutalized by want, and children robbed of their childhood shall be things of the dark past."

In his four years as editor of the *Post*, George continued to round out editorially his social philosophy and his political economy while launching many campaigns to save California from the power of special interests which ranged from police corruption to liquor licensing. And while no abuse of public trust was small enough to escape his notice, he was the first to recognize the greater issues when they arose. The "Christian republic" of which he dreamed could be established only through progress that did away with poverty. After leaving the *Post* on November 27, 1875, George was able once again to reflect upon the "enigma" of the times, the "riddle which the Sphinx of Fate puts to our civilization, and which not to answer is to be destroyed." The problem was to introduce his major work four years later, but the problem and the symbolism in which it was expressed harked back to the "millennial" letter he wrote to his sister in 1861.

IV *Preludes to* Progress and Poverty

George's career in the 1870's can be divided into two distinct periods of almost equal length: 1871 to 1875, and 1875 to 1879. In the first period, his time was almost entirely devoted to his successful newspaper career as editor of the San Francisco *Post*. In the second, it was given to reflection and to the composition of *Progress and Poverty*. The decade is bracketed by his first extended statement on political economy, *Our Land and Land*

Policy (1871), and by the lectures and essays of the late 1870's which lead on to his major work completed in the spring but not published until the fall of 1879.

Our Land and Land Policy attempted at least a brief answer to the Sphinx. Coming as it did almost halfway between his letter of 1861 and the beginning of his international career as the "Prophet of San Francisco," *Our Land and Land Policy* is an important step in George's intellectual development. The pamphlet (dated July 27, 1871) was actually a forty-eight-page booklet expanded from an earlier version of thirty-one pages. It was closely printed and vigorously argued, sold for twenty-five cents, and contained a folding map of California showing the land grants made to the railroad. Though he was already theorizing on an international scale, the booklet was clearly aimed at national, state, and local problems.

Our Land and Land Policy is divided into five parts, each with subsections: (1) "The Lands of the United States," (2) "The Lands of California," (3) "Land and Labour," (4) "The Tendency of Our Present Land Policy," and (5) "What our Land Policy Should Be." Parts three and five present the essentials of the argument he develops fully in *Progress and Poverty*: the land monopolizers and speculators or owners of large tracts obtain the majority of the benefits of economic progress; if they were heavily taxed, most social problems would be solved. Parts one, two, and four were aimed at careless state and national policies that were causing economic waste, sapping natural resources, and irresponsibly concentrating landownership in the hands of the relatively few.

George's distributist doctrine and the tone of *Progress and Poverty* are already in evidence in *Our Land and Land Policy*. Once more the reader may observe the Emersonian Sphinx metaphor:

> There is a problem which must present itself to every mind which dwells upon the industrial history of the present century; a problem into which all our great social, industrial, and even political questions run—which already perplexes us in the United States; which presses with still greater force in the older countries of Europe; which, in fact, menaces the whole civilized world, and seems like a very riddle of the Sphinx, which fate demands of modern civilization, and which not to answer is to be destroyed —the problem of the proper distribution of wealth.[14]

His basic Jeffersonian philosophy is proclaimed earnestly, provocatively, and with Jeffersonian rhetoric:

> But man has also another right, declared by the fact of his existence [in addition to his right to the fruits of his own labor] —the right to the use of so much of the free gifts of nature as may be necessary to supply all the wants of that existence, and as he may use without interfering with the equal rights of any one else, and to this he has a title as against all the world.
>
> This right is natural; it cannot be alienated. It is the free gift of his Creator to every man that comes into the world—a right as sacred, as indefeasible as his right to life itself.[15]

George was going to end poverty by ending the monopoly of land. The land belonged to everybody to use freely, and once this "natural right" was abridged dire consequences inevitably resulted. What is more, monopoly meant class division, and ultimately inequality and class war. The greater the concentration of wealth, the poorer the majority of people became. Such developments meant the end of Democracy, the destruction of the Republic, and the re-establishment of the Old World in the New. Shortly after publishing *Our Land and Land Policy*, George began publishing the *Post*. It was only after he left the paper in 1875 that he was able to return to these ideas at greater length than editorials would permit.

His series of addresses in 1877 and 1878 are important because they began his career as a speaker and contributed to the development of his style. They also illustrate his growing awareness of his personal mission. Whereas in 1871, after having published *Our Land and Land Policy*, he had written on a particular matter in the *Overland Monthly*, "Bribery in Elections," from 1877 through 1879 he philosophized on a broader base. In 1871 he attacked corruption at the polls, railroad money in the elections, and advocated the Australian ballot system in order to insure privacy at voting places through compulsive security and official government ballots. At the end of the decade, he was concerned with economic theory and its practical application throughout the world.

In 1877, he wrote two important speeches. The first was read at the University of California, then established permanently at Berkeley, and was entitled "The Study of Political Economy."

The second was his Fourth of July oration. Referring to Adam Smith, Ricardo, and Mill in the university address, George spoke sharply and suggestively. He had some vague hopes that perhaps he was destined for the unfilled chair of political economy at the university, but he surely must have expected as little academic enthusiasm for his opinions on political economy as for his ideas on education:

> Education is not the learning of facts; it is the development and training of mental powers. All this array of professors, all this paraphernalia of learning, cannot educate a man. They can but help him to educate himself. Here you may obtain tools; but they will be useful only to him who can use them. A monkey with a microscope, a mule packing a library, are fit emblems of the men—and, unfortunately, they are plenty—who pass through the whole educational machinery, and come out but learned fools, crammed with knowledge which they cannot use—all the more pitiable, all the more contemptible, all the more in the way of real progress, because they pass, with themselves and others, as educated men.

Such was the way the self-educated George spoke at Berkeley. Formal educational institutions and Henry George were never destined to get on well with one another. Even at the height of his popularity in the United Kingdom, George suffered at Oxford University one of his rare failures. Though he became a very effective speaker in later years and could move an audience, it was in general an audience who labored with body and soul in order to live and who had known starvation. These were the audiences who responded to him in the spirit in which he addressed them. His success with radical intellectuals depended upon their already developed sympathies with human suffering and want which were similar to his own.

George's Fourth of July oration, "The American Republic," was an apotheosis of Liberty. He was at his rhetorical best, but had still to learn that an effective speaker cannot simply talk *at* an audience. The language of the address, however, was the language of his later speeches and essays. In the speech he briefly reviewed the rise of liberty in the Judaic ethic and its progress through Christian and European history. At the same time, he referred to land and labor problems, emphasizing the injustice of the concentration of wealth, the degradation of the poor, and the loss of freedom through economic bondage. "In the long run," he said, "no nation can be freer than its most oppressed, richer than its poorest, wiser than its most ignorant." "The ultimate condition of any people," he said, "must be the condition of its lowest class."

Two other essays, "Why Work Is Scarce, Wages Low, and Labour Restless" and "Moses" were written while he was already at work on *Progress and Poverty*. The first of these two statements of his views anticipates in much detail the chapter "The primary cause of recurring paroxysms of industrial depression" in Book V of *Progress and Poverty*, but "Moses" carries in essence the entire spirit as well as much of the substance of George's appeal. Describing the purpose of "Why Work is Scarce," George wrote to John Swinton that the essay was "an attempt to put into popular form a great truth which marries political economy with common sense, and which once appreciated is the key to all the social evils of our time." "Moses," on the other hand, was a declaration of his mission to the world and a personal and national statement of the American Dream.

George first delivered his lecture on Moses in June, 1878, to the Young Man's Hebrew Association in San Francisco. Though he may have felt the power of the prophet stirring within him when he interrupted his labors on his major work, he was as well prepared as he ever would be to express the essence of the message he was to amplify later in the many books and speeches. "Moses" is a succinct enunciation of his social philosophy, and rising as it did out of the great heat generated by the composition of *Progress and Poverty*, it has much in common with that book: both are prophetic in tone and both are addressed to the same problem.

In "Moses," George examines the enigma of poverty amidst plenty specifically in terms of the ethical and moral foundations of Western society, and he does so in keeping with a theme that recurs throughout nineteenth-century literature from Coleridge and Carlyle to Emerson and Arnold—the hero and his relation to culture and anarchy. If, George says, "we try to trace to their sources movements whose perpetuated impulses eddy and play in the currents of our times, we at last reach the individual. It is true that 'institutions make men,' but it is also true that 'in the beginnings men make institutions.'" For George, Moses is a culture hero, a representative man, whose biography he describes in transcendental terms.

"Moses" is a provocative address, and it can be understood why George repeated it in Scotland, England, and New York. It is Emersonian, not simply because George had read Emerson from his youth, but because it is a poetic essay strikingly like a sermon. But it is also Emersonian because it is devoted to the American Dream of the individual in a *New* England instead of an *Old* England. The modern world, and specifically America, George conceived as unlimited in its potential: a veritable promised land was inevitably to rise out of the wilderness of technological achievement. Only the inability of men to understand what Thoreau or Jefferson knew could bar the way: the land belonged to everybody, to the people as a whole, and must not fall into the hands of private ownership; for the land is man's only because God has given, perhaps lent, it to him. It belongs to *all* men as children of God, and it is to be forever held in usufruct for all of the people: "Everywhere in the Mosaic institutions is the land treated as the gift of the Creator to His common creatures, which no one had the right to monopolise. Everywhere it is, not your estate, or your property, not the land which you bought, or the land which you conquered, but 'the land which the Lord thy God giveth thee'—'the land which the Lord lendeth thee.'" To George, who had witnessed the deeding of lands to the Central Pacific and the actions of countless land speculators in California, only economic and moral disaster could be the ultimate result:

> Trace to its root the cause that is thus producing want in the midst of plenty, ignorance in the midst of intelligence, aristocracy in democracy, weakness in strength—that is giving to our civilization a one-sided and unstable development, and you will find it something which this Hebrew statesman three thousand years ago perceived and guarded against. Moses saw that the real cause of the enslavement of the masses of Egypt was, what has everywhere produced enslavement, the possession by a class of the land upon which and from which the whole people must live. He saw that to permit in land the same unqualified private ownership that by natural right attaches to the things produced by labour, would be inevitably to separate the people into the

very rich and the very poor, inevitably to enslave labour—to make the few the masters of the many, no matter what the political forms; to bring vice and degradation, no matter what the religion.

The lesson of "Moses" is based upon "the idea of the brotherhood of men" which "springs from the idea of the fatherhood of God"; for "the great distinctive feature of the Hebrew religion . . . is its utilitarianism, its recognition of divine law in human life." Moses had "a character blending in highest expression the qualities of politician, patriot, philosopher, and statesman," which re-educated and led his people from a slave psychology to that of a free people. In the characteristic fashion of the American writer, George, like Melville or Whitman, sees America repeating the experiences of the Israelites. By implication, he sees another Exodus from the old to the new, and he even draws the attention of his audience to the parallel experience of the small tribe of colonials who sought a new land of milk and honey in the wilderness of the New World. "Egypt was the mould of the Hebrew nation—the matrix, so to speak, in which a single family, or, at most, a small tribe grew to a people as numerous as the American people at the time of the Declaration of Independence."

Like the founders of America, again by implication, Moses sought no glory for himself but desired that specific safeguards be made against the foundation of any kind of hereditary succession. "As we cannot imagine the Exodus without the great leader, neither can we account for the Hebrew polity without the great statesman. Not merely intellectually great, but morally great—a statesman aglow with the unselfish patriotism that refuses to grasp a sceptre or found a dynasty." When a people have become free both in mind or spirit and in body, the function of the code they live by is to protect this hard-won freedom, to make the enslavement of the past impossible in the present or in the future of that people: "It is not the protection of property, but the protection of humanity, that is the aim of the Mosaic code. Its sanctions are not directed to securing the strong in heaping up wealth so much as to preventing the weak from being crowded to the wall. At every point it interposes its barriers to the selfish greed that, if left unchecked, will surely differentiate men into landlord and serf, capitalist and workman, millionaire and tramp, ruler and ruled."

"The aim of the Mosaic code is," says George, "a commonwealth based upon the individual—a commonwealth whose ideal it was that every man should sit under his own vine and fig tree, with none to vex him or make him afraid." Above all, the Mosaic code is a safeguard against economic enslavement. The Sabbath is the sign that none are "condemned to ceaseless toil." Pressing his point, George will not let his audience forget the harsh realities of the nineteenth century:

> We progress and we progress; we girdle continents with iron roads and knit cities together with the mesh of telegraph wires; each day brings some new invention; each year marks a fresh advance—the power of production increased, and the avenues of exchange cleared and broadened. Yet the complaint of "hard times" is louder and louder; everywhere are men harassed by care, and haunted by the fear of want. With swift, steady strides and prodigious leaps, the power of human hands to satisfy human wants advances and advances, is multiplied and multiplied. Yet the struggle for mere existence is more and more intense, and human labour is becoming the cheapest of commodities. Beside glutted warehouses human beings grow faint with hunger and shiver with cold; under the shadow of churches festers the vice that is born of want.

George was positive that he was ethically and morally right, and therefore economically sound and socially just. "I ask," he said in "Moses," "not veneration of the form, but recognition of the spirit" of the Mosaic institutions:

> How common it is to venerate the form and deny the spirit. There are many who believe that the Mosaic institutions were literally dictated by the Almighty, yet who would denounce as irreligious and "communistic" any application of their spirit to the present day. And yet to-day how much we owe these institutions! This very day the only thing that stands between our working classes and ceaseless toil is one of these Mosaic institutions. Nothing in political economy is better settled than that under conditions which now prevail the working classes would get no more for seven days' labour than they now get for six. . . .
> Let the mistakes of those who think that man was made for the Sabbath, rather than the Sabbath for man, be what they

may; that there is one day in the week that the working man may call his own, one day in the week on which hammer is silent and loom stands idle, is due, through Christianity, to Judaism—to the code promulgated in the Sinaitic wilderness.

George's views were based upon the traditional Protestant and democratic spirit of dissent and rebellion against tyranny. And it was these views that had made him defend the execution of Emperor Maximilian of Mexico years earlier. Like Milton, he believed it to be the right of the people to depose the unrepresentative and unjust tyrannies of the princes of this world. Regicide was not only defensible but even laudable.[16] Moses is seen to be the prime author, in spirit at any rate, of the Declaration of Independence:

> From the free spirit of the Mosaic law sprang that intensity of family life that amid all dispersions and persecutions has preserved the individuality of the Hebrew race; that love of independence that under the most adverse circumstances has characterised the Jew; that burning patriotism that flamed up in the Maccabees and bared the breasts of Jewish peasants to the serried steel of Grecian phalanx and the resistless onset of Roman legion; that stubborn courage that in exile and in torture held the Jew to his faith. It kindled that fire that has made the strains of Hebrew seers and poets phrase for us the highest exaltations of thought; that intellectual vigour that has over and over again made the dry staff bud and blossom. And passing outward from one narrow race it has exerted its power wherever the influence of the Hebrew scriptures has been felt. It has toppled thrones and cast down hierarchies. It strengthened the Scottish covenanter in the hour of trial, and the Puritan amid the snows of a strange land. It charged with the Ironsides at Naseby; it stood behind the low redoubt on Bunker Hill.

At the beginning of his newspaper career, George wrote for a short while under the pseudonym of "Proletarian"; and when he was speaking in the British Isles in the 1880's, he spoke as a proletarian against vested interests, both clerical and lay. The "unholy alliance" he called it. The "harlot's curse," to borrow a phrase from the verse of a native English proletarian of the previous century, was on England, and George never let his audiences forget it. The "squalor and brutishness with which the very centres of our civilisation abound" was impossible to defend. The audiences that heard the "Moses" address in Dundee in February, 1884, or in Glasgow the following December heard George at his best. "The life of Moses, like the institutions of Moses, is a protest against that blasphemous doctrine, current now as it was three thousand years ago—that blasphemous doctrine preached oft-times even from Christian pulpits—that the want and suffering of the masses of mankind flow from a mysterious dispensation of providence, which we may lament, but can neither quarrel with nor alter." There was no doubt about who was to inherit the earth. There was no doubt about what "self-evident" truths were being preached. The opposition recognized a familiar voice. "We hardly know where to begin in pointing out the fallacies in a train of reasoning which starts from the assumption that all men are created equal and ends with the conclusion that private property in land is a monopoly in some sense which distinguishes it from private property of other kinds."[17] Henry George was preaching an unwanted democratic socialism based upon the American Declaration of Independence so far as his opposition was concerned.

In "Moses" George set the whole tone and direction of his social and economic reevaluation of modern society. "It was no sudden ebullition of passion that caused Moses to turn his back," like Milton's Christ, on all the glories of the Egyptian and Grecian worlds. Moses brought his "strength and knowledge . . . to the life-long service of the oppressed." "In institutions that moulded the character of a people, in institutions that this day make easier the lot of toiling millions, we may read the stately purpose."

George returned to his desk in order to finish *Progress and Poverty. Our Land and Land Policy* at the beginning of the decade and the four essays of the last three years of the 1870's were only preludes to it. George, like Moses, had a dream of a land of plenty in which there was to be neither poverty nor slavery and where each man was to be his own master.

CHAPTER *3*

Progress and Poverty:
A Solution to an Enigma
Addressed to the World

I *The Publication of* Progress and Poverty

PROGRESS AND POVERTY was the summing up of Henry
George's California experience; and though it was not until
the fall of 1879 that it appeared in print, George's diary indicates
that a completed manuscript was sent to New York in March of
the same year. The diary also tells us that he had "Commenced
Progress and Poverty" two years before in September, 1877.
Much of the United States was then suffering from the effects of
an economic depression, a condition that still prevailed generally
in 1879. Strikes and riots were not infrequent. In many states
troops were under arms, and in California the decline in the ship-
ments of silver from the Comstock Lode and the winter drought
led to increased unemployment, reduced wages, and a general
decline of stocks. George himself was in debt. During the spring
and summer of 1877, he delivered those lectures (including the
University of California speech) which no doubt confirmed his
long-standing plans to write a book on economic conditions and
political objectives.

Essentially fruitless activity with the Land Reform League
was the only real interruption in his intense labors on *Progress
and Poverty,* since his occasional speeches and lectures served to
warm him to his task. For a year and a half at least, he worked
steadily on the manuscript. When it was finished in March,
1879, George found that he could not secure a publisher who
would agree to publish a long treatise on political economy. Nobody guessed that *Progress and Poverty* was to be the *Uncle*

Tom's Cabin of the 1880's. Certainly for a book on political economy its unparalleled success was not only unanticipated but also astounding. Like Mrs. Stowe's novel, *Progress and Poverty* was addressed to the question of slavery—economic or wage slavery. And the landowner and monopolist were the Simon Legrees of the piece.

According to his diary, George sent a copy of the manuscript of *Progress and Poverty* to Appleton & Co., in New York on March 22, 1879, because he did not believe any of the firms on the West Coast were prepared to handle the book. Also since Appleton published books and series of books on philosophy, science, and economics, like those of Herbert Spencer, whom George had read and considered to have influenced him, he sent the manuscript to the East. However, it was declined, George receiving word by mid-April. Soon Harper's and Scribner's joined Appleton by rejecting it also.

Having taken to heart the advice that it would be impossible to find a publisher willing to print the book unless the author provided the plates himself, George, with no money but with the help of his old partner and friend, Hinton, began setting the type in mid-May. Such an arrangement made it convenient for him to revise his work as the type was being set, and the book's style and organization were generally improved. By the late summer a small "Author's Edition" of five hundred copies was printed and distributed. Sending a copy to his father in Philadelphia, George wrote prophetically and emotionally, "It represents a great deal of work and a good deal of sacrifice, but now it is done. It will not be recognized at first—may be not for some time—but it will ultimately be considered a great book, will be published in both hemispheres, and be translated into different languages. This I know, though neither of us may ever see it here."[1]

Two weeks later Appleton wrote George that it had reconsidered and would be willing to publish the book now that the author could supply the plates. George had sent unbound copies of the "Author's Edition" to a number of publishers in both England and the United States as soon as they had come off the press, but Appleton was the only one that made him a proposal. They said they would issue it at once at two dollars a copy with a royalty of fifteen per cent to the author. Appleton scheduled the New York Edition for the following January (1880). George's relief matched his satisfaction. In a letter to a friend in the East, George wrote about the book with the same confidence he had displayed in his letter to his father:

> If the book gets well started, gets before the public in such a way as to attract attention, I have no fear for it. I know what it will encounter; but, for all that, it has in it the power of truth. When you read it in its proper order and carefully, you will see, I think, that it is the most important contribution to the science of political economy yet made; that, on their own ground, and with their own weapons, I have utterly broken down the whole structure of the current political economy, which you so truly characterise. The professors will first ignore, then pooh-pooh, and then try to hold the shattered fragments of their theories together; but this book opens the discussion along lines on which they cannot make a successful defence.[2]

While awaiting possible publication of *Progress and Poverty* in the spring of 1879, George had begun a weekly called *The State*, which ran only eleven issues and which had to be abandoned in order to give him the necessary time to work on his author's edition through the summer. It was the second paper he had started after having left the *Post*. In 1875 he had begun the *Ledger*, a small morning daily with an illustrated Sunday edition which he also had to abandon because he tried to publish it without seeking advertisements; he had hoped that advertisers would seek out the paper once they recognized its worth. Needless to say, its existence was short-lived.

In *The State* he had written, "Are men free when they have to strain, and strive, and scheme, and worry, to satisfy the mere animal wants of life? Are men free when, pressed by the fear of want, they are forced to starve their higher natures and to tread under foot, in the fierce struggle for wealth, love, honor, justice and mercy?" To these questions he addressed *Progress and Poverty*. "It is the institutions of man, not the edicts of God that enslave men," he wrote. "It is the greed and ignorance of mankind, not the niggardliness of nature that show themselves in poverty and misery, and want-produced vice. Yet while we prate of freedom, we strangle freedom; while we thank God for liberty, we load liberty with fetters."[3] Such sentences express the spirit, style, and diction of *Progress and Poverty*. Henry George's plea for social reform was gaining clarity and strength.

Given the conditions of the time and the hope to which he gave voice, George was soon to find a vast audience ready to listen. His hope and his vision were irresistible, and they reflected the general utopian dreams of many late nineteenth-century essays and books as much as they described the need for social reform that also characterized a large body of the literature of the same period. John Dewey has said that George was "typically American" and that his philosophy was a kind of "Practical Idealism." But though the first description is indeed correct, the second can be misleading. George's philosophy can only be called "Practical Idealism" if one understands, as Dewey does, that it is a *practical* program that depends upon man's good will for its success. That is why George has had many adherents but never the majority of opinion necessary to put his program into action on a large scale. The "Practical" becomes *impractical* if we do not share George's "Idealism." His views require a faith of a very special kind, which he briefly expressed in his lecture on Moses. His economic reforms are part of the "full sweep" of his ideas.

Dewey goes on to say that "In spite, therefore, of the immense circulation of George's writings, especially of *Progress and Poverty* (which I suppose has had a wider distribution than almost all other books on political economy put together), the full sweep of George's ideas is not at all adequately grasped by the American public, not even by that part which has experienced what we call a higher education. Henry George is one of a small number of definitely original social philosophers that the world has produced."[4] In writing of this "great intellectual loss," Dewey says that he is speaking only of "acquaintance" with George's ideas "irrespective of adoption or nonadoption" of his policies. Dewey's observations are those of a student of social philosophy some fifty years after the fact.

But even if a modern reader were as sympathetic to some of George's views as Dewey was, George's success in his own time was due to facts and factors that are not explicit in his work when it is studied for itself in academic isolation—even by an objective student of political economy. The influence George had upon his readers can never be traced solely to his political economy. In the 1880's *Progress and Poverty* had the effect of a bible, and George often had the impact of a prophet. Furthermore, accepting George's views, even in part, meant first sharing his informed optimism and his idealism rather than his pragmatism. The practicality of his program, no matter how convincing in and by itself, demanded an idealistic view of man and that was why he was to run afoul of both the political conservative and the doctrinaire socialist.

II *The Form and Style of* Progress and Poverty

The fundamental character of *Progress and Poverty* is to be found in its attempt to harmonize the individualism of capitalist economics with the communalistic goals of Christian charity, and the form that it takes is basically related to George's idealistic and pragmatic effort to solve an enigma even greater than that of the ironically parallel advance of poverty and progress which he considered the problem of the times. This duality has been recognized by some of George's best critics who trace his sensitivity to this dilemma to both his heritage and his knowledge of Thomas Henry Buckle's *History of Civilization,* in particular the "Examination of the Scotch Intellect during the Eighteenth Century" to which George refers at the beginning of his refutation of Malthus in *Progress and Poverty* (Book II, Chapter I):

> Commenting on Adam Smith, the historian noted that the great economist had written his two treatises from quite separate premises about human nature and had never reconciled them. "In his *Moral Sentiments,* he ascribes our actions to sympathy; in his *Wealth of Nations,* he ascribes them to selfishness." Buckle explains that Smith wrote with one hand as though men lived in great and religious concern with affairs outside themselves, and so evoked the highest principles and the deepest emotions; with the other hand he wrote as though self-seeking were the only motive in the world.[5]

The duality of *Progress and Poverty* is sustained throughout the book's twelve divisions. The "Introductory" section, "The Problem," begins the critique by asserting that the "association of poverty with progress is the great enigma of our times." It is the current form of the "riddle which the Sphinx of Fate puts" to all civilizations. Modern economic theory must deal with the sharp "contrast between the House of Have and the House of Want"; otherwise "progress is not real and cannot be permanent." The book's "Conclusion," "The Problem of Individual Life," ends with an allusion to "Christian and Faithful" making their way "through the streets of Vanity Fair" while "clanging blows" ring "on Great Heart's armor." The quest for economic and moral justice is none other than that in which the Parsees of old were involved. "Ormuzd still fights with Ahriman—the Prince of Light with the Powers of Darkness."

Like Melville at one moment, like Whitman the next, George seeks to "utter the word Democratic, the word En-Masse," yet to sing of the "simple separate person." George creates an analogical structure for *Progress and Poverty* whereby he is able to oscillate continually from socio-economic questions to religio-philosophic truths, and from revolutionary collectivistic reforms to evolutionary individual development. This oscillation is fundamental to the form or structure of George's argument and carries the weight of his pragmatic and idealistic solution to the problem he has posed for the reader. Neither the pragmatic nor the idealistic half of the solution is sufficient in itself—both are necessary. The "Problem" and "The Problem of Individual Life" must be solved together. The final form of the full title of his book indicates what he had in mind with regard to the general problem: *Progress and Poverty/An Inquiry into the Cause of Industrial Depressions and of Increase Of Want with Increase of Wealth/The Remedy.*

Progress and Poverty is divided into twelve parts: an introduction, ten books, and a conclusion. It is a long critique, and in the twentieth century it has often been condensed. As a rule, these condensations spring from efforts to extract the fundamental ideas of George's theory and to disentangle his hard-headed practicality from his Victorian rhetoric and nineteenth-century idealism at the cost of the over-all effect of the original.

Unlike the true socialist, if George can be called a socialist at all, he is not committed to either Hegelian dialectics or to historical and materialistic determinism. He can believe in progress without absolute assurance, and he can also be pessimistic without despair. Though he incorporates some of Spencer's early ideas on land reform, which twelve or thirteen years later George attacked him for abandoning, he rejects the English philosopher's Social Darwinism. Though indebted to the tradition of "natural rights," so often associated with Rousseau, George's Christian bias, with its Jeffersonian and transcendental, often Emersonian, vision, is at odds with the agnosticism of the age— at odds with Thomas Huxley as much as with Marx, both of whom were as hostile to George as he was to them. His attack upon Spencer in 1892 and Spencer's opinion of George, together with other politically conservative assaults, indicate how great the personal and philosophical antipathies were. They also indicate how often the supposedly "practical" men—the real pragmatists of the time—gathered together in opposition to George.

Progress and Poverty is as much a book of an American Protestant reformer as it is anything else, and thus he was to have as much trouble with the Roman Catholic Church (though his wife was reared in the Church and though a priest was to be one of his chief supporters in New York) as he was to have with the agnostic materialists. When in the years to come he was to call Spencer the "Pope of the Agnostics," after his long struggle with Rome in the late 1880's, it is easy to see that George had understood that his Christianity and romanticism (or idealism) had been rejected by the materialists as completely as his theories for social reform had been rejected by the largest of Christian churches.

Yet the form and style of *Progress and Poverty*, aside from its arguments, could not be what it is had not George believed in the harmony of a religious commitment and social reform. That is why his lecture on Moses is important to George's writing and to his program. Beyond acknowledging the fact that Moses had led the Jews into a life which was devoted to socio-economic and religio-philosophic unity—a kind of total ethics—George also expressed his belief that in Moses' vision the individual was neither glorified at the expense of others nor determined by his past history of enslavement. Man was not only free to choose, to make history rather than be a victim of it, but he was also free of any kind of determined biological process of evolution. He was chosen by God, not selected by nature. In his own way, George tried to lean politically left and spiritually right.

George's style reflects the time in which he wrote and also his newspaper training. Occasionally it is Emersonian, transcendental, oracular, and aphoristic. He is given to illustrative quotations, eclectic allusions, specific examples, and concrete images. He sermonizes and engages in poetic flights. *Progress and Poverty* was a lively book in its day, and its success was largely due to its rhetorical sincerity. Reading it was like touching a man. It certainly was a kind of "song of myself." It betrays its California origins and its author's heritage, but it is universal in its appeal. And one of the reasons it was a convincing statement of its author's ideas was that its universality was rooted in particulars. George's lucid logic always serves his vigorous analysis. His own commitment is so great that, once the reader accepts his primary ideas, George becomes almost irrefutable. Therefore, despite its vast amount of detail and its lack of twentieth-century tables of statistics, *Progress and Poverty* is still as effective, if not so convincing, as it once was. Its symmetry and basic simplicity gives a kind of literary class that most books on essentially non-literary subjects lack. George is a near perfect illustration of Emerson's aphorism in *The Poet*, "The man is only half himself, the other half is his expression." *Progress and Poverty* is like its author: its argument is only half itself; the other half is its expression.

George's expression of his own personality is to be found elsewhere than in the expressed argument of the book. At the beginning of every major division in *Progress and Poverty*, George inserts a favorite or appropriate quotation that reflects his own commitment to man's struggle for dignity, freedom, and justice. In this effort to indicate that he is not alone in what he demands, he includes selections from Marcus Aurelius, Edwin Arnold, Whittier, De Tocqueville, Tennyson, Mrs. Browning, Sir William Jones, Ptolemy, Carlyle, Montesquieu, Milton, Isaiah, Themistocles, and others. Many of the same writers are quoted in the text. Strung together, however, the quotations become a small anthology of social commentary by themselves and serve as a kind of esthetic accompaniment to the references to Mill, Malthus, Spencer, Adam Smith, Ricardo and others who are more fully a part of the political and economic arguments in the text.

George's choice of the title *Progress and Poverty* also indicates his newspaperman's sense of the simple yet memorable phrase. His abilities as a promoter of causes and as an effective propagandist, however, were always beyond question. His most formidable opponents always acknowledged that, if nothing else. He knew that his tentatively alternate title, "Political Economy of the Social Problem" would not do. It had to be "Progress and Poverty," despite the appearance of the alternate title on the flyer he distributed in order to announce his forthcoming "Author's Edition."

No matter what the title or how symmetrical the form, *Progress and Poverty* is a nineteenth-century book. Its style and its length are often too rich, too prolix, and too much for the twentieth-century reader; but then the same has been said of Carlyle, of Emerson, of Ruskin, and, for that matter, of Marx. In its own time, however, it was very widely read—an all-time best seller by modern standards. It is still far from being a dead book. A well-expressed missionary zeal is often irresistible, especially when it seeks to remedy obvious wrongs by a cogent criticism of them. Poverty still afflicts the affluent society almost one hundred years after George had said he had found the remedy. He argued the American Dream, but he also sought its fulfillment.

III   *The Content of* Progress and Poverty: *Argument, Philosophy, and Prophecy*

The argument of *Progress and Poverty*, like the form, is based upon the book's duality and the author's attempt to resolve that duality. It was a duality, however, that the author did not invent but only emphasized. Beginning in the "Introductory" with the assertion "That political economy, as at the present taught, does not explain the persistence of poverty amid advancing wealth in a manner which accords with deep-seated perceptions of men" (12-13),[6] George devoted the first two books of his critique (one-fourth its entire length) to refutations of (1) the wages-fund theory of employment, and (2) the Malthusian theory of population. He held both theories responsible for society's failure to recognize clearly or deal effectively with the problem of the times.

George attacked the wages-fund theory because it enslaved the wage-earner and empowered the employer by making employment depend upon "existing capital." In a series of propositions that denied "the teachings of the current political economy," George said that wages were paid *after* labor had been performed and *after* the products of labor had been placed upon the market. Therefore, he reasoned, wages were paid by labor itself out of its own investment of effort and did not reduce the capital funds of the employer. He said that it was the "demand for consumption," or the needs of the people, that really employed labor. Such a point of view led him to deny Malthus' theory of population and to assert subsequently that labor employs capital, capital does not employ labor. This reversal of the normal assumptions of his time became one of the main arguments of Book V, "The Problem Solved."

Essentially, George had reversed himself. He had used the theories he now rejected to support in part his opposition to Chinese immigration. His attack upon them in *Progress and Poverty* was detailed and vigorous. By saying that the wages-fund theory depressed wages to the subsistence level, he cleared the ground for his rejection of Malthus. He argued that the more people that were employed, the greater they increased production and capital. Not only did the quantity of the products increase to fill the demand, but so did the quality. Paid a proper living wage, the wage-earner would consume the products of his own labor and demand more: "If each laborer in performing the labor really creates the fund from which his wages are drawn, then wages cannot be diminished by the increase of laborers, but, on the contrary, as the efficiency of labor manifestly increases with the number of laborers, the more laborers, other things being equal, the higher should wages be" (88).

To George's mind, Malthus flew in the face of logic and observable fact. Famine and underfed peoples were as common in underpopulated areas of the world, such as Brazil, as they were in overpopulated areas, such as Ireland. Vice and misery could be traced to exploitation, to war, to tyranny, and to oppression, but not to overpopulation:

Twenty men working together will, where nature is niggardly, produce more than twenty times the wealth that one man can produce where nature is most bountiful. The denser the population the more minute becomes the subdivision of labor, the greater the economies of production and distribution, and, hence, the very reverse of the Malthusian doctrine is true; and, within the limits in which we have reason to suppose increase would still go on, in any given state of civilization a greater number of people can produce a larger proportionate amount of wealth, and more fully supply their wants, than can a smaller number. (149-50)

Whatever *"does* produce poverty amid advancing wealth," George concluded, it is not overpopulation. That we do not lack the productive power necessary, he also argued, has been proven by our ability to produce continually all kinds of accumulated wealth through labor alone:

Take wealth in some of its most useful and permanent forms— ships, houses, railways, machinery. Unless labor is constantly exerted in preserving and renewing them, they will almost immediately become useless. Stop labor in any community, and wealth would vanish almost as the jet of a fountain vanishes when the flow of water is shut off. Let labor again exert itself, and wealth will almost as immediately reappear. This has been long noticed when war or other calamity has swept away wealth, leaving population unimpaired. (148)

The groundwork had been laid for his investigation of "The Laws of Distribution" in Book III. Classical economics, dependent upon the Malthusian and the wages-fund theories, could not explain, much less solve, the enigma of poverty amidst progress. Having defined his terms in Book I, George was prepared in Book III to begin discussing immediately the problems of distribution. He had said that the three "factors of production" were land, labor, and capital; and to these were related the three elements of distribution—rent, wages, and interest. Land combined with labor to create wealth. Capital was taken from produced wealth, previously accumulated through labor, and returned to production to create additional wealth. Advantageous sites, as in the mining industries in California, George assigned as rent to the landowner rather than as wage to the worker because they were uncreated wealth:

Land, labor, and capital are the factors of production. The term land includes all natural opportunities or forces; the term labor, all human exertion; and the term capital, all wealth used to produce more wealth. In returns to these three factors is the whole produce distributed. That part which goes to land owners as payment for the use of natural opportunities is called rent; that part which constitutes the reward of human exertion is called wages; and that part which constitutes the return for the use of capital is called interest. These terms mutually exclude each other. The income of any individual may be made up from any one, two, or all three of these sources; but in the effort to discover the laws of distribution we must keep them separate. (162)

George applied " 'Ricardo's law of rent,' " describing it as follows: *"The rent of land is determined by the excess of its produce over that which the same application can secure from the least productive land in use"* (168). In recapitulation, therefore, he said that "in algebraic form: As Produce = Rent + Wages + Interest . . . Produce — Rent = Wages + Interest. . . . Thus wages and interest do not depend upon the produce of labor and capital, but upon what is left after rent is taken out; or, upon the produce which they could obtain without paying rent—that is, from the poorest land in use. And hence, no matter what be the increase in productive power, if the increase in rent keeps pace with it, neither wages nor interest can increase" (171).

George reveals his essentially non-Marxist view by suggesting that workers and investors have a common cause against the landowners, landholders, and land speculators, that workers were not alone in a struggle with the united force of landowners and investors (the "capitalists" of socialism). In fact, George went on to say, the investor was also a kind of wage-earner, just as the laborer was himself an investor: by their combined efforts the value of the land was increased, but only the landowner benefited from the increase.

The chapters on capital and interest in Book III indicate that he takes pains to defend interest-taking, though he had rejected one of the major tenets of eighteenth- and nineteenth-century capitalism: the wages-fund theory of employment. George defended interest on the basis of his California experiences, using the development of the land in the mining industry as an example. Expenses legitimately spent in such betterment of the land deserved a return on the investment costs. To make his position clear, George included a chapter on "Of Spurious Capital and of Profits often mistaken for Interest." Monopolies, such as those in transportation and communication, George characteristically decried. He suggested once again, as he had earlier as a newspaper editor, that they should be owned and operated, if not built, by the government. He defended the "law of interest," defining it as follows: *"The relation between wages and interest is determined by the average power of increase which attaches to capital from its use in reproductive modes. As rent arises, interest will fall as wages fall, or will be determined by the margin of cultivation*" (203). He compared the "True Statement" on rent, wages, and interest with what he called the "Current Statement" as follows:

The Current Statement	The True Statement
RENT depends on the margin of cultivation, rising as it falls and falling as it rises.	RENT depends on the margin of cultivation, rising as it falls and falling as it rises.
WAGES depend upon the ratio between the number of laborers and the amount of capital devoted to their employment.	WAGES depend on the margin of cultivation, falling as it falls and rising as it rises.
INTEREST depends upon the equation between the supply of and demand for capital; or, as is stated of profits, upon wages (or the cost of labor), rising as wages fall, and falling as wages rise.	INTEREST (its ratio with wages being fixed by the net power of increase which attaches to capital) depends on the margin of cultivation, falling as it falls and rising as it rises. (219)

He summed up his argument by returning to his favorite theme, the land question. "And, hence, that the increase of productive power does not increase wages, is because it does not increase the value of land. Rent swallows up the whole gain and pauperism accompanies progress. . . . To see human beings in the most abject, the most helpless and hopeless condition, you must go, not to the unfenced prairies and the log cabins of new clearings in the backwoods, where man single-handed is commencing the struggle with nature, and land is yet worth nothing, but to the great cities, where the ownership of a little patch of ground is a fortune" (224).

The key to George's critique was his characteristic distinction between used and unused land, land in production and land purposely held out of production by speculators waiting for progress to make them rich through rent. A continual conflict— a kind of economic war—could always be expected between unearned income (rent), which was made at the expense of others, and labor-earned income (wages and interest), which ironically at its own cost gave the land its new and ever-increasing value.

Book IV begins George's program for the confiscation of rent for the benefit of the many instead of the few. This section is based largely on all the specific attacks he had made on particular persons and interests in his California editorials. However, in *Progress and Poverty*, George impersonalizes his argument. Though a twentieth-century economic critic would produce statistical evidence in support of its ideas and conclusions, George does not. After all, he felt the statistics were self-evident and available to everyone as they had been to him. Instead, he takes a transcendental tone and launches into long paragraphs that describe the "virgin and rich" soil, the glories of "Nature . . . at her very best," and the immigrant's struggle to settle and to build upon the land that has been freely given by nature to him and not to the monopolist. He describes the effect of a new and increasing population on the distribution and creation of wealth and the subsequent increase of rent.

After stressing labor's improvement of the land and the progress that results from its inventiveness, he closes Book IV by returning once again to the causes of "the steady increase of rent, . . . speculation, or the holding of land for a higher price than it would . . . otherwise bring" (255). "The influence of speculation in land in increasing rent is a great fact which cannot be ignored in any complete theory of the distribution of wealth in progressive countries. It is the force, evolved by material progress, which tends constantly to increase rent in a greater ratio than progress increases production, and thus constantly tends, as material progress goes on and productive power increases, to reduce wages, not merely relatively, but absolutely" (259). "If," however, "the corrupt governments of our great American cities were to be made models of purity and economy, the effect would simply be to increase the value of land, not to raise either wages or interests" (254). In Book IV he supports the arguments of Book III by citing and examining actual conditions and by relating them to the laws of distribution that depend upon the conflict between rent *and* wages and interest.

Book V, "The Problem Solved," concentrates on the reasons for recurrent depressions and poverty amid progress by harmonizing the themes and ideas that arise from books III and IV. The first of its two chapters, "The Primary Cause of recurring Paroxysms of Industrial Depression," places the blame not on rent in itself but on captured rent: wealth taken out of production. Land monopoly in particular and all forms of monopoly in general are said to be the major causes of economic disasters. "The speculative advance in rent, or the value of land, which produces the same effects as (in fact, it is) a lock-out of labor and capital by landowners. This check to production, beginning at the basis of interlaced industry, propagates itself from exchange point to exchange point, cessation of supply becoming failure of demand, until, so to speak, the whole machine is thrown out of gear, and the spectacle is everywhere presented of labor going to waste while laborers suffer from want" (270).

The second chapter, "The Persistence of Poverty amid advancing Wealth," stresses the importance of the land itself: "the habitation of man, the storehouse upon which he must draw for all his needs." Therefore, the monopolizers of land enslave labor. "That as land is necessary to the exertion of labor in the production of wealth, to command the land which is necessary to labor, is to command all the fruits of labor save enough to enable labor to exist" (294). His conclusions are as obvious as they are consistent with his California experiences and his editorial views on land policy. "Material progress cannot rid us of our dependence upon land; it can but add to the power of producing wealth from land; and hence, when land is monopolized, it might go on to infinity without increasing wages or improving the condition of those who have but their labor" (296). The possession of land gives power to the landholder: "Everywhere, in all times, among all people, the possession of land is the base of aristocracy, the foundation of great fortunes, the source of power" (296).

Reaching the mid-point of his critique, and having already made good use of De Tocqueville, George concludes Book V with a literary allusion that is a propagandistic gem, one magnificently apt and powerfully Emersonian: "As said the Brahmins, ages ago—'To whomsoever the soil at any time belongs, to him belong the fruits of it. White parasols and elephants mad with pride are the flowers of a grant of land.'" George's style and argument come together: in order to enjoy its fruits, the people must repossess the land from the new aristocracy of wealth just as surely as they had once taken it from an old aristocracy of birth that had sprung from an even older aristocracy of wealth.

Like Book V, Book VI, "The Remedy," is also divided into two significant chapters: "Insufficiency of Remedies currently

[74]

advocated," and "The True Remedy." This second chapter is only a little over two pages and is by far the briefest in *Progress and Poverty*. In rejecting current remedies, George organizes his argument in terms of six general ideas: (1) greater economy in government; (2) better education of the working classes and improved habits of industry and thrift; (3) combinations of workmen for the advance of wages; (4) co-operation of labor and capital; (5) governmental direction and interference; and (6) a more general distribution of land.

His major views include: (1) opposition to personal income tax because it would discourage incentive; (2) support of trade unions of skilled laborers because they would lower profits and increase wages at the expense of rent—he opposed the large international unions of unskilled labor that the socialists proposed; (3) arguments against the effects of strikes because to him they destroyed "personal freedom." "The man who would fight for freedom, must, when he enters an army, give up his personal freedom and become a mere part in a great machine, so must it be with workmen who organize for a strike. These combinations are, therefore, necessarily destructive of the very things which workmen seek to gain through them—wealth and freedom." Such views and his defense of interest-taking indicate how far removed George was from socialist habits of thought.

Nevertheless, George's sympathies are clear; he is no conservative. His economic romanticism is no more strongly in evidence than in his explicit comments upon socialism and in his emphasis upon the organic nature of society as opposed to the mechanistic. Because of this concept, George often compares the current economic conditions he describes to a machine that is not functioning properly. The point is, of course, that the society he seeks cannot be manufactured. "The ideal of socialism is grand and noble; and it is, I am convinced, possible of realization; but such a state of society cannot be manufactured—it must grow. Society is an organism, not a machine. It can live only by the individual life of its parts. And in the free and natural development of all the parts will be secured the harmony of the whole." In an apotheosis, he concludes, "All that is necessary to social regeneration is included in the motto of those Russian patriots sometimes called Nihilists—'Land and Liberty'" (321). He ends *Progress and Poverty* in essentially the same way.

Though "The True Remedy" is only two pages, George, in fact, reduces the chapter to one italicized sentence: *"We must make land common property."* In "nothing else is there the slightest hope." With his "remedy" for an already well-described need finally stated, George then prepared to justify it. Books VII and VIII are devoted, respectively, to the "justice" of the remedy and to its "application." Quickly following up his solution, he writes in the first chapter of Book VII that "The equal right of all men to the use of land is as clear as their equal right to breathe the air—it is a right proclaimed by the fact of their existence. For we cannot suppose that some men have a right to be in this world and others no right" (338). In a sense this justification is an outgrowth of his Jeffersonian and Emersonian points of view as much as the inevitable development of his argument. In "The True Remedy," he writes that "The laws of the universe are harmonious," for "if the remedy to which we have been led is the true one, it must be consistent with justice . . . must accord with the tendencies of social development and must harmonize with other reforms" (329). His discussion of "the enslavement of laborers," which he believed was "the ultimate result of private property in land," went so far as to conclude that "Private ownership of land is the nether millstone. Material progress is the upper millstone. Between them, with an increasing pressure, the working classes are being ground" (357). George did not believe that they were the millstones of the gods but the creations of a sick economy.

George does not agree that compensation is justified when the land is made common property, for the private appropriation was originally an unjust social development. Furthermore, it is not a thing of the past: the "robbery" of the land is a continuing injustice which the people as a whole continue to suffer. Therefore, if the landowners wish to retain possession of the land presently held in their names, they must return the rent to the community. That is why he writes in Book VIII that *"It is not necessary to confiscate land; it is only necessary to confiscate rent."* In any case, the land belongs to the whole community. In confiscating the rent the people are merely reclaiming what has been taken from them unjustly. Such confiscation, therefore, is the righting of a wrong and not an injustice: "I do not propose either to purchase or to confiscate private property in land. The first would be unjust; the second, needless. Let the individuals who now hold it still retain, if they want to, possession of what they are pleased to call *their* land. Let them continue to call it *their* land. Let them buy and sell, and bequeath and devise it. We may safely leave them the shell, if we take the kernel" (405). The confiscation of rent calls for a reformed system of taxation, and that, in fact, is how George intends to apply his "true remedy":

> What I, therefore, propose, as the simple yet sovereign remedy, which will raise wages, increase the earnings of capital, extirpate pauperism, abolish poverty, give remunerative employment to whoever wishes it, afford free scope to human powers, lessen crime, elevate morals, and taste, and intelligence, purify government and carry civilization to yet nobler heights, is—*to appropriate rent by taxation.*
>
> In this way the State may become the universal landlord without calling herself so, and without assuming a single new function. . . . and every member of the community would participate in the advantages of the ownership.
>
> Now, insomuch as the taxation of rent, or land values, must necessarily be increased just as we abolish other taxes, we may put the proposition into practical form by proposing—
>
> *To abolish all taxation save that upon land values.* (405-6)

Though the phrase was not used, George had laid down the principles of "the single tax" with which he was forever to be associated.[7]

In the final two chapters of Book VIII, he defended his tax system and tried to show its advantages. Book IX, therefore, carries the discussion of advantages from questions of economic wealth to those of individual and social betterment. In many ways it prepares the reader for George's version of the American Dream and a world-wide utopia. In his last two books and in his conclusion, George makes every effort possible to convince his reader that his reforms will fulfill his dream and bring that utopia into being; but, while Book IX sums up his socio-economic ideas, it is Book X and the conclusion that bear the weight of his religio-philosophic eloquence.

Though George's statements would not have the effect today that they had in 1879—despite current concern with the persistence of poverty—they were extremely convincing. George had begun his treatise on a moral point, and he skillfully returned to it at the end. Book X goes a long way toward merging his socio-economic and pragmatic ideas with his religio-philosophic and idealistic views. It is a consolidation of the random utopian views George had expressed in many of his *Post* editorials. In fact, with the coda-like "Conclusion," Book X bears comparison with the many utopian romances that were popular in the final decades of the nineteenth century, not to mention books like Blatchford's *Merrie England*. Charles Barker makes a very important observation of the way in which *Progress and Poverty* is brought to a close:

> Once more *Progress and Poverty* moves carefully, and keeps a little apart from English thought, and especially from moral tones of social Darwinism. The book goes a certain distance again, indeed, with the age's most prominent social thinker, then qualifies as follows: "That civilization is an evolution—that it is in the language of Herbert Spencer, a progress from indefinite, incoherent homogeneity to a definite, coherent, heterogeneity—there is no doubt; but to say this is not to explain or identify the causes which forward or retard it." In complete moral dissent from dominant British and German habits of thought, George entered the opinion that the age's inclination to justify overseas expansion, as though the name of evolution and the science of Darwin made right the exploiting of weak peoples, had encouraged a hateful racism and nationalism.[8]

Because George clearly preferred the organic to the mechanical or automatic, he considered *true* progress, like the "true remedy," to be neither inevitable nor necessary: it was hopefully possible, but it was dependent upon man's moral and intellectual growth. His proposal was neither British nor Germanic: it was American. He makes very cogent historical observations, ones more perceptive than the comment on Spencer which Barker quotes.

> It cannot be said of the Hindoo and of the Chinaman, as it may be said of the savage, that our superiority is the result of a longer education; that we are, as it were, the grown men of nature, while they are the children. The Hindoos and the Chinese were civilized when we were savages. They had great cities, highly organized and powerful governments, literatures, philosophies, polished manners, considerable division of labor, large commerce, and elaborate arts, when our ancestors were wandering

barbarians, living in huts and skin tents, not a whit further advanced than the American Indians. While we have progressed from this savage state to Nineteenth Century civilization, they have stood still. If progress be the result of fixed laws, inevitable and eternal, which impel men forward, how shall we account for this? (482)

The clarity and essential rightness of his insights into historical processes and the rise and fall of civilizations do George credit, especially when one considers that the popular view of his era tended to place Victorian man at the pinnacle of an ever-developing civilization. It is not easy to refute George's *"universal rule"*: "But it is not merely these arrested civilizations that the current theory of development fails to account for. It is not merely that men have gone so far on the path of progress and then stopped; it is that men have gone far on the path of progress and then gone back. It is not merely an isolated case that thus confronts the theory—*it is the universal rule*. Every civilization that the world has yet seen has had its period of vigorous growth, of arrest and stagnation; its decline and fall" (484). Along with his Spenglerian anticipations, George held fast to his idea that "it becomes possible for man to improve only as he lives with his fellows. All these improvements, therefore, in man's powers and conditions we summarize in the term civilization. Men improve as they become civilized, or learn to co-operate in society" (477).

George returns to the manner and message of "Moses" in the last one hundred pages of *Progress and Poverty*. Basing his point of view once again on the living Hebraic vision of equality, freedom, and justice for all men (and contrasting it again with the dead Egyptian past), he says that American democracy and Christian faith are vitally necessary to secure a truly progressive society. The Hebraic-Christian democratic vision almost demands that the land be *common* property and that social classes be dissolved: "Civilization is co-operation. Union and liberty are its factors. [524] . . . the law of human progress . . . proves that the making of land common property . . . would give an enormous impetus to civilization, while the refusal to do so must entail retrogression. A civilization like ours must either advance or go back; it cannot stand still" (527).

George's utopian dream is not a blind one. "How Modern Civilization may Decline," Chapter IV of Book X, is often Orwellian. "Now this transformation of popular government into despotism of the vilest and most degrading kind, which must inevitably result from the unequal distribution of wealth, is not a thing of the far future. It has already begun in the United States, and is now rapidly going on under our eyes" (533). "Whence shall come the new barbarians?", he asks. "Go through the squalid quarters of great cities, and you may see, even now, their gathering hordes!" He asks: "How shall learning perish?" And he prophetically replies: "Men will cease to read, and books will kindle fires and be turned into cartridges!." The optimism of *Progress and Poverty*, which often seems overwhelming, is tempered by a Jeremiah-like prophetic tone. As Emerson suggests it should have, George's goodness has an edge to it—and in public debate it could be cutting.

"The Central Truth," the concluding chapter of Book X, is almost entirely comprised of George's July Fourth, 1877, San Francisco oration on Liberty. Only the first six short paragraphs are new, and they are centered on the "self-evident" truths of the Declaration of Independence to which George again, as always, returns. His apotheosis to Liberty is carried over to the "Conclusion," "The Problem of Individual Life." To this problem of individual life, "the meaning of life—of life absolutely and inevitably bounded by death," he relates equally the facts and themes of his politico-economic critique and the "myth and symbol," "type and allegory" of "ultimate relations"—the Garden of Eden, the laborers in the vineyard. Apprehension of the "primary truth," George believed, was the chief end of all life. His own transcendental gleam did not blind him to the kind of needless suffering that can itself blind the sufferers.

George's attempt to move his reader completely was most successful because he did not hesitate to say that the social organization in its neglect of *all* the people stood in the way not only of spiritual but of material progress. Many who read George's book as a testament of freedom sensed that he wrote not for progress' sake but for their sake. "We are apt to assume," he wrote in Book IX, "that greed is the strongest of human motives, . . . that the fear of punishment is necessary to keep men honest—that selfish interests are always stronger than general interests" (457). "Nothing could be further from the truth," he wrote in confrontation of the basic duality of the book. George had always to deal with the alternative motives behind the acts of man which Buckle attributed to Adam Smith: that man acted towards his brother either from sympathy or from selfishness.

But if man were poor, what could he do but seek in every just way to rid himself of his hated impoverished condition. Those who are struggling merely to exist on the animal level cannot afford the luxury of sympathy which seems denied them even by those who can truly afford it. But *want* and the fear of poverty in those who *have* is the real economic basis for self-seeking. The progress of a nation and the poverty of its people make "civilized existence an Ishmaelitish warfare."

> Carlyle somewhere says that poverty is the hell of which the modern Englishman is most afraid. And he is right. Poverty is the open-mouthed, relentless hell which yawns beneath civilized society. And it is hell enough. The Vedas declare no truer thing than when the wise crow Bushanda tells the eagle-bearer of Vishnu that the keenest pain is in poverty. For poverty is not merely deprivation; it means shame, degradation; the searing of the most sensitive parts of our moral and mental nature as with hot irons; the denial of the strongest impulses and the sweetest affections; the wrenching of the most vital nerves. (457)

"From this hell of poverty, it is but natural that men should make every effort to escape," says George (458). Since all men tend to admire what they desire, fear of poverty makes them "admire above all things the possession of riches." Naturally, they will live their lives according to "the lesson that society is daily and hourly dinning in the ears of its members": "Get money—honestly, if you can, but at any rate get money!" (459).

George's belief that spiritual progress must accompany material progress is given added emphasis in the "Conclusion." Immortality is not an opiate so far as George is concerned; it is what is at stake. No one who could have insisted so completely as George did that the land was by right the common property of the people could have failed to understand the sacramental meaning of life on the land or of the nature of life itself. George would have understood the teaching of Martin Buber, the modern Jewish theologian, just as well as he had understood

Moses. The conclusion of *Progress and Poverty* is in mood and meaning in harmony with his lecture "Moses," just as the final chapter of Book X is literally his oration on Liberty. The genesis of each characteristic is identical with that which George thought was the "great distinctive feature of the Hebrew religion . . . its utilitarianism, its recognition of divine law in human life." We may recall his comment on the "grand and noble . . . ideal of socialism" that is "possible of realization," the growing social organism that lives "only by the individual life of its parts": "All that is necessary . . . is . . . 'Land and Liberty.' " In beginning with the economic "problem" that beset society as a whole, he had to end with "the problem of individual life." Discussing or attempting to solve one meant discussing or attempting to solve the other. Neither the "dismal science" ("Political Economy") nor the *dismal life* was by divine decree so ordained.

IV   *Contemporary Reactions to* Progress and Poverty

George sent a number of complimentary copies of the "Author's Edition" of *Progress and Poverty* to prominent persons, including William Gladstone and Herbert Spencer in England, the Duke of Argyll in Scotland, and Sir George Grey in New Zealand. Gladstone sent a courteous but neutral acknowledgment which said, in part, that there was "no question which requires a more careful examination than the land question in this and other countries, and I shall set great store on whatever information you may furnish under this head."[9] The Duke of Argyll, in whom George mistakenly sensed liberal tendencies, graciously acknowledged receipt of the gift; but several years later he and George clashed with international bitterness over the very questions raised in *Progress and Poverty*. Spencer made no reply at all, but some time later both he and George were to denounce one another. Of the four, only Grey responded enthusiastically. "I have already read a large part of the book," he wrote, and "regard it as one of the ablest works on the great questions of the time, which has come under my notice." "It has cheered me much," he went on, "to find that there is so able a man working in California, upon subjects on which I believe the whole future of mankind now mainly hangs."[10]

The California papers were, of course, among the first to comment upon the book of their fellow citizen and newspaper colleague, and naturally enough they were divided in their opinions. The *Alta California* said the book would be "dropped out of view in a short time as a blunder of a mind more active than wise."[11] But the Sacramento *Record-Union,* in one of the longest of the early reviews, thought it "a very remarkable book" that was "destined to have a very great success."[12] The book was written in a fine style, the *Record-Union* said, and "its sincere sympathy with humanity, its tenderness, its passionate desire for better things" would commend it to the "average mind." The paper, nevertheless, was critical of George's basic ideas and took issue with his attack on Malthus, giving him a chance to reply (on March 13, 1880),[13] which as always he gladly accepted as another opportunity to spread his gospel. The San Francisco *Chronicle* said that "notwithstanding the comparative obscurity of this writer as compared with Ricardo, Adam Smith, Mill, Spenser [*sic*] and others on the same subject, his volume will attract much attention among advanced minds."[14] Those reviews that were completely favorable were often written by friends and associates, like Dr. E. R. Taylor, who praised the book in the *Californian* after having read it in manuscript while helping to see it through the press.

Most eastern reviews were at first cool and noncommittal, but they generally felt that the book was unusual and provocative. The *Popular Science Monthly,* owned by Appleton, George's publisher, helped to publicize *Progress and Poverty* by first printing in its March, 1880, issue George's University of California lecture, "The Study of Political Economy," and then by saying in its April review that *Progress and Poverty* was a "remarkable answer" and "one of the most important contributions yet made to economic literature." In March, The New York *Sun's* reviewer, M. W. Hazeltine, wrote about the book at great length, saying that George's "conclusions, however strange and revolutionary they may seem in their bearing upon society, will not be rejected by sober and impartial men without mature deliberation." No matter how opposed or antagonistic, he wrote, "they cannot afford to neglect his plea or ignore his argument. . . . Few books have, in recent years, proceeded from any American pen which have more plainly borne the marks of wide learning and strenuous thought, or which have brought to the expounding of a serious theme a happier faculty of elucidation."[15] George was much moved and gratified by this review, coming as it did almost exactly a year after he had first sent the manuscript to Appleton's.

Other eastern papers began to respond. The radical *Irish World*, with which George in the year to come was to have much to do, gave *Progress and Poverty* a generally favorable review, but it thought George's views were not sufficiently socialistic. The New York *Times*, then a relatively new Republican paper, rejected it almost out of hand. These two reviews indicate to what extremes reactions to George were to go in the future. About the same time the reviews in the *Irish World* and the *Times* appeared, the *Nation* published a concise but serious and detailed review of the book, giving it a thoughtful and scholarly examination. It was, however, a general dissent from George's economic ideas, making little or no comment upon his religio-philosophic views. In this way the *Nation's* review was the very opposite of that of the *Christian Register*, the leading Unitarian journal in Boston, which stressed George's Christian charity and religious concern for "the world's misery." By fall, the *Atlantic Monthly* had joined the steady parade of reviewers by giving it a double review. The two writers, interestingly enough, stressed different sides of the book; and while one argued against the economic analysis, the other faintly praised its suggestions for the betterment of the wage-earner.

The academic and orthodox criticism of George's book was not long in coming, and it was inevitably hostile. Since George had attacked some of the most cherished notions of economic theory, the counterattack was often virulent. Professor W. G. Sumner's review in the June, 1881, number of *Scribner's Monthly* stated that it was unfortunate indeed that the same "respectful attention" was "given to a book like this" that was also given "to the most careful work of a highly trained and scientific observer." The point of view of the entire review was that George was untrained and unqualified for the task he had set himself. In Sumner's opinion, the book misrepresented and misunderstood more than it clarified; and he mourned the fact that "Sociology" was still "the free arena for all the people with hobbies, crude notions, world philosophies, and 'schemes.'" In short, Sumner thought *Progress and Poverty* a basically dangerous book. He certainly did not give it the "sober attention" the New York *Herald* thought it deserved from "our leading political economists"; for Sumner wrote:

> It has been declared several times, in regard to Mr. George's "Progress and Poverty," and by various reviewers, that its appearance marks an epoch or constitutes an event. We are cordially of the same opinion, although for a somewhat different reason. Nothing could more distinctly mark the absence of any true body of criticism in social science and political economy than the respectful consideration which has been given to this book. It now appears in paper covers in a popular edition, and is going on its way to propagate still more social folly and prejudice where already there is so much that common sense scarcely has a chance.[16]

George's brief and provocative *The Irish Land Question* had just been published, and Sumner condemned it also. Opinions such as these were echoed later by others, especially after George had been to the British Isles and had actively contributed to movements for economic and political reform.

Besides the reviews, the reactions of individuals to George's book indicated that its world-wide fame was already in the making. Dr. Montague Leverson, a student of Mill, called *Progress and Poverty* "*the* book of the half-century"; and Alfred Russel Wallace, the famous English biologist, who was himself a leading Land Nationalist, said the book was "undoubtedly the most remarkable and important work of the present century."[17] The popularity of *Progress and Poverty* and the fame of its author, however, were yet to reach their peak.

One of George's closest friends of long standing, John Russell Young, who had gone early in 1880 to London with several copies of *Progress and Poverty*, which he distributed to Members of Parliament, tried again unsuccessfully to secure a position for George with the New York *Herald*. Young's reactions to George's character during this period, which he recalled in the New York *Herald* at the time of George's death in the fall of 1897, are particularly illuminating because he was one of the few men long close to George who never fully shared his views: "George never for a moment—never when under the grinding heel of bitter conditions—doubted the truth of his mission to mankind and its ultimate success. The more I studied George under heavy conditions the more I admired him. His ability and his courage; his honesty, independence, and intellectual power were those of a leader of men. . . . It was the courage which, as has been written, makes one a majority."

This assessment of George's character has the ring of and, in fact, alludes to the words of Thoreau. George in 1880 was still a prophet keenly aware of his mission who was without a people; and he was also a man with a family who had an economic theory but little or no personal economic stability. Though financial difficulty was nothing new to George, he was clearly intent on surviving as a majority of one who knew he had God on his side. In 1881 on a short trip to California, the "majority of one" was beginning to prevail. At the Metropolitan Temple, where three years before he had spoken to a "beggarly array of empty benches," he now confronted a crowded auditorium. Even the *Alta California*, who had dismissed his book "as a blunder," referred to him as the "author of 'Progress and Poverty,' a book that has made him a great name as a political economist."[18] Now that he had returned to California in modest triumph after having been in the East for a year or so, he was soon to turn to the British Isles in order to follow up in person the appearance there of his recent *Irish Land Question* and of the British edition of *Progress and Poverty*.

Kegan Paul in London, which had agreed in 1880 to publish the English edition of *Progress and Poverty*, brought out the first printing the same year. It was exhausted by early 1881. Because of George's visits to the British Isles in 1881-82 and 1883-84, the book sold at a phenomenal rate, soon going into a special sixpenny edition. Having once thought very little of its possibilities, George's British publisher soon had great expectations for *Progress and Poverty*.

By 1884 all the major British papers and journals of international repute had reviewed *Progress and Poverty*, and George felt that now he was to get the proper judgment, favorable or not, that was generally denied him in the United States. The book was reviewed at length by the London *Times*, as well as by the most famous British periodicals of the nineteenth century: the *Contemporary Review, Quarterly Review, Edinburgh Review*, and *Nineteenth Century*.

Though *Progress and Poverty* had been reviewed unfavorably

earlier (1881) in England in the *Economist* and in the *Statist*, the *Times* did not comment until George's activities in Ireland had brought him personal notoriety. In September, 1882, the *Times* printed a letter he had written to the paper that called for moderation in Ireland. The *Times* made a long editorial comment on his opinions and activities, which recognized fairly that George was a power on the political scene, but which asserted no sympathy for his program or for his views. The *Times* placed him and the Land Nationalization movement in the same category as it did the socialists and communists. Despite this obviously unfavorable editorial opinion, the formal review of *Progress and Poverty*, including some commentary on *The Irish Land Question* (published in 1881 and selling even better than *Progress and Poverty*), was a fair and almost neutral assessment of the book. With good reason, its conclusions pleased George immensely:

> Mr. George's idea will long be found in the book only; nevertheless, "Progress and Poverty" well merits perusal. It contains many shrewd suggestions, and some criticisms of economic doctrines which future writers on political economy must either refute or accept. Mr. George's reading has evidently been wide; he has reflected deeply; he is an acute reasoner, and he is the master of an excellent style. The readers of his book may dissent from his statements and conclusions, without regretting the time they have spent over it; and, if conversant with economic doctrines and interested in the problems of social science, they will find in its pages much to ponder with care and much that is highly suggestive.[19]

The earliest and perhaps the most interesting of the reviews in the periodicals was that of Emile de Laveleye in the *Contemporary Review*. Two years before de Laveleye had reviewed *Progress and Poverty* in *La Revue scientifique*. He now tempered his earlier praise (not qualified) by carefully charting what he thought were George's unsocialistic errors, such as the pro-capitalistic justification of interest and investment returns. He also criticized George for what he considered an inadequate argument against the wages-fund theory. He praised George for his attack on Malthusianism and for his application of Ricardo's law of rent.

The *Quarterly Review* printed an out-and-out denunciation of

George's book, written almost as a pronouncement for class prejudice:

> If we may credit a leading Radical journal, it [*Progress and Poverty*] is fast forming a new public opinion. The opinion we here allude to is no doubt that of the half-educated; but this makes the matter in some ways more serious. No classes are so dangerous, at once to themselves and to others, as those which have learned to reason, but not to reason rightly. . . . They will fall victims to it [a false economic theory], as though to an intellectual pestilence. Mr. George's book is full of this kind of contagion. A ploughman might snore, or a country gentleman smile over it, but it is well calculated to turn the head of an artizan. . . . It is not the poor, it is not the seditious only, who have thus been affected by Mr. George's doctrines. . . . They have been gravely listened to by a conclave of English clergymen. Scotch ministers and Nonconformist professors have done more than listen—they have received them with marked approval; they have even held meetings, and given lectures to disseminate them. Finally, certain trained economic thinkers, or men who pass for such in at least one of our Universities, are reported to have said that they see no means of refuting them, and that they probably mark the beginning of a new political epoch.[20]

The review was a call to arms. The reviewer was not interested in "false theories" in and for themselves nor in "How they shake the wise," which he felt was "a matter of small moment." The "great question," he said, was "how they will strike the ignorant." The book and its author were clearly dangerous threats to the established order.

Under the title "The Nationalization of Land," the *Edinburgh Review* reviewed Herbert Spencer's *Social Statics* and *Progress and Poverty* together, though the former had been published in 1850. Again George was praised for his application of Ricardo's law and for his attack on Malthus, but he was sharply criticized for his distributionist ideas and for his land taxation schemes. His work was considered to be a part of the "revolutionary warfare now waged by certain Americans, or Hiberno-Americans, against the institutions of this country, which degrades them to the level of the Socialists of Germany, the Nihilists of Russia, and the Communards of Paris."[21]

All in all, the British reviews treated *Progress and Poverty* as a book that had to be taken seriously and examined thoroughly.

The *Modern Review* even went so far as to say that the book was to be recommended for its timeliness and for its views on land taxation, a strong indication that the reviewer was not a Tory, as were the reviewers in the *Edinburgh Review* and the *Quarterly Review*.

Needless to say, in little more than five years *Progress and Poverty* had become a world book. Reviews, like de Laveleye's in *La Revue scientifique* and the *Contemporary Review*, had appeared in England and on the Continent, the first in France in 1881. One of his German reviewers had said that *Progress and Poverty's* "author is an uncommonly gifted thinker." By 1886 translations had appeared in German, French, Swedish, Danish, Norwegian, and Dutch; it was soon translated into Spanish, Italian, Hungarian, Russian, Bulgarian, Chinese, and Yiddish. For a 563-page book on political economy (its length in the standard edition), the success of *Progress and Poverty* was unparalleled. The workingmen of many nations responded by willingly reading a long book on a theoretical subject from cover to cover (probably for the first time) because they sensed that at last one of their own was putting their case before the world. Their support was as enthusiastic as it was great in number.

CHAPTER 4

The Yankee Prophet "Over There":
News from the New World to the Old

I   The Irish Land Question *and* Social Problems

IN THE EARLY 1880's George published two books, *The Irish Land Question* (1881) and *Social Problems* (1883). Both works were related to his journalistic activities, to his first two visits to the British Isles, and to *Progress and Poverty*. *The Irish Land Question* (subsequently reprinted simply as *The Land Question*) grew out of an article for the Sacramento *Bee's* Christmas issue in 1879. When George again took up the question over a year later, the article developed into a book of seventeen short chapters of roughly one hundred pages. Less philosophic than *Progress and Poverty*, the book's full title, *The Irish Land Question, What It Involves and How Alone It can be Settled,* indicates its pragmatic attempt to treat a specific economic condition.

The book is addressed to a typical Georgian rhetorical question: "What would the Irish landlords lose, what would the Irish tenants gain, if, tomorrow, Ireland were made a State in the American Union and American law substituted for English law?" George wrote the "little book, or rather pamphlet" to help introduce his ideas into Ireland in the midst of the unrest there. Michael Davitt, one of the Irish leaders, came to New York in 1880 to gather support for the Irish Land League. After meeting George, Davitt agreed to publicize *Progress and Poverty* when he returned home. Thinking the book too complicated and theoretical for use as propaganda within the Irish Land League, George decided to write a statement of his views suitable for the membership. Appleton immediately agreed to publish the new book.

The Irish Land Question became popular almost at once, and George achieved his purpose. The book, basically an introduction to his economic remedy, is only moderately concerned with Ireland in particular; but George is very critical of Parnell's theories and policy. Essentially, George uses the Irish condition as a prime example of the need for reform, and he presents in simple terms his arguments for the confiscation of rent and the return of the land to all the people. The captured rent, he says, should be returned to the whole community in the form of very much needed social services. Emphasizing his usual universal appeal to the workingman and the landless, he calls upon the people of Ireland to join with their English brethren in their fight for independence. The condition of labor, he argues, is just as bad throughout the world as it is in Ireland, if not worse:

> What I urge the men of Ireland to do is to proclaim, without limitation or evasion, that the land, of natural right, is the common property of the whole people, and to propose practical measures which will recognize this right in all countries as well as in Ireland.
> What I urge the Land Leagues of the United States to do is to announce this great principle as of universal application; to give their movement a reference to America as well as to Ireland; to broaden and deepen and strengthen it by making it a movement for the regeneration of the world—a movement which shall concentrate and give shape to aspirations that are stirring among all nations. (106-7)[1]

George concluded the book with his usual quotation from the Declaration of Independence about self-evident truths and equality, never popular ideas with England's governing classes.

The Irish Land Question was of great personal value to George. It advertised *Progress and Poverty*, increased its author's notoriety, and prepared the ground for his visit to Ireland as a special correspondent of the *Irish World*. In fact, after George arrived in the British Isles, he found that the British edition of *The Irish Land Question* was selling even better than *Progress and Poverty* while also increasing the sales of the larger book. He was correct, therefore, in assuming that the smaller work would make its readers want to study *Progress and Poverty*. The "universal question" was the question that counted the most, and *The Irish Land Question*, like *Our Land and Land Policy*, simply illustrated this point by examining a particular local condition which reflected the universal one.

The Irish Land Question was often reviewed with *Progress and Poverty*. In George's support of the Land Nationalization movement in England and in his plans to "start the revolution," the smaller book functioned like a destroyer escort convoying a battleship of the line into a decisive engagement for the control of the economic seas over which the British Empire had ruled unchallenged by wandering Yankees demanding their "inalienable rights." The two books and George in person made their major impact on England, Ireland, and Scotland by arraigning the claims of English, Irish, and Scottish landlords with "the widespread institution of private property in land" which George asserted was "the great social problem of modern civilization" (21-22).

Social Problems, coming shortly after, summed up effectively —both in the United States and in the United Kingdom—the collectivistic side of George's social remedy. It sold well on both sides of the Atlantic and reflected his experiences in New York City between his first two trips to the British Isles; but it also indicates how conscious he was of the distress he had witnessed abroad.

Social Problems is a compilation of twenty-two chapter-articles, thirteen of which appeared in *Frank Leslie's Illustrated Newspaper*. The articles were written indirectly as a response to the opinions of Professor William Graham Sumner who had just published a series of articles in *Harper's Weekly* and who had so harshly reviewed *Progress and Poverty* in *Scribner's Monthly* about two years before. The *Leslie* essays were published under the general title "Problems of the Times" and appeared throughout the spring and summer of 1883.

Social Problems marks an interesting change of emphasis in George's work. In his discussion of collectivistic measures needed for social reform, he stressed the importance of public ownership and government control of monopoly in industry. Though based upon *Progress and Poverty, Social Problems* was addressed more directly than George's major work to industrial questions and to public utility problems that beset large cities, especially in the northeastern United States. In a prefatory note, George said that he had tried to "present the momentous social problems of our time, unencumbered by technicalities and without that abstract reasoning which some of the principles of political economy require for thorough explanation." He referred to *Progress and Poverty*, saying he was discussing points "not touched upon, or but slightly touched upon" in the earlier work; however, he also referred his reader to it for fuller discussion of related ideas.

George's reputation was in the process of change when he was engaged in writing *Social Problems*. He was becoming less the respected author and more the social agitator. His opponents often attempted satire and ridicule in order to lessen the influence he was having on public opinion; even *Leslie's* felt obliged to accompany his series of articles with criticism of the author on its editorial page. Nevertheless, George's influence could not be wished away, and a review of *Social Problems* in the New York *Independent* for May 1, 1884 (just about a year after the "Problems of the Times" began to appear in *Leslie's*), reinforced its continuing presence: "Henry George exercises a strong influence over a vast number of people. We must face the fact squarely, whether we like it or not. His books are sold and read in America and England as no other books are sold and read; the sales are numbered by the hundred thousand, the readers by the million."

Social Problems has remained George's most bluntly socialistic book. Coming as it did between his first two visits to the British Isles and reflecting his personal commitment to active reform movements, its socialistic character is everywhere in evidence. His statement on "the truth in socialism" in Chapter XVII expresses sharply his views on the purpose of government:

> The primary purpose and end of government being to secure the natural rights and equal liberty of each, all businesses that involve monopoly are within the necessary province of governmental regulation, and businesses that are in their nature complete monopolies become properly functions of the state. As society develops, the state must assume these functions, in their nature cooperative, in order to secure the equal rights and liberty of all. That is to say, in the process of integration, the individual becomes more and more dependent upon and subordinate to the all, it becomes necessary for government, which is properly that social organ by which alone the whole body of individuals can act, to take upon itself, in the interest of all, certain functions

which cannot safely be left to individuals. Thus out of the principle that it is the proper end and purpose of government to secure
the natural rights and equal liberty of the individual, grows the
principle that it is the business of government to do for the mass
of individuals those things which cannot be done, or cannot be
so well done, by individual action. As in the development of
species, the power of conscious, coordinated action of the whole
being must assume greater and greater relative importance to the
automatic action of parts, so is it in the development of society.
This is the truth in socialism, which, although it is being forced
upon us by industrial progress and social development, we are so
slow to recognize. (176-77)

He went on to say in the same chapter that "the natural progress
of social development is unmistakably toward cooperation, or,
if the word be preferred, toward socialism, though I dislike to
use a word to which such various and vague meanings are attached" (191). George's meaning was clear no matter what word
he chose to use. The "welfare state" was just exactly what George
expected the state to be. The public was responsible for the
welfare of its members; and when private interests did not contribute to the welfare of individuals, it was the duty of government to intercede on their behalf.

George's comments upon the rights of man and economic
slavery in chapters X and XV are powerfully provocative. Besides
effectively introducing the principle that those who owned the
land owned the people on it, his comments upon *Robinson Crusoe*
(his favorite book) at the beginning of Chapter XV also indicate that as a literary critic George was capable of important
insights. Defoe's social criticism, implied and explicit, in *Robinson Crusoe* was not lost upon George.

> Robinson Crusoe, as we all know, took Friday as his slave.
> Suppose, however, that instead of taking Friday as his slave,
> Robinson Crusoe had welcomed him as a man and a brother;
> had read him a Declaration of Independence, an Emancipation
> Proclamation and a Fifteenth Amendment, and informed him
> that he was a free and independent citizen, entitled to vote and
> hold office; but had at the same time also informed him that
> that particular island was his (Robinson Crusoe's) private and
> exclusive property. What would have been the difference? Since
> Friday could not fly up into the air nor swim off through the

sea, since if he lived at all he must live on the island, he would have been in one case as much a slave as in the other. Crusoe's ownership of the island would be equivalent to his ownership of Friday. (148-49)

It was an especially effective example, particularly for the English, Scottish, and Irish readers. Of course, exempla of this sort are the hallmark of George's style and also the reason why he could be so moving as a writer and a speaker.

Before he had organized his material into book form, a job on which he was still at work just before his second departure for the British Isles in December, 1883, the series of articles in *Leslie's* cost him additional time and effort. In his fifth essay he had provoked a controversy from which he was to triumph personally and which may well have helped to sell copies of the book itself. "The March of Concentration," which is also the fifth chapter of *Social Problems*, is concerned with the concentration of population in cities and of land in fewer hands. In it, George took on another Yale University professor of economics, General Francis A. Walker, a more prominent figure in his day than W. G. Sumner. George had known Walker's work from an earlier date. He had referred approvingly to *The Wages Question* in *Progress and Poverty* and, in fact, did not seek the quarrel that ensued. Walker had just become president of the Massachusetts Institute of Technology. He was president of the American Statistical Association, was soon to be president of the American Economics Association, and had been a director of the United States Census. In his "Compendium of the Tenth Census," Walker had said that the average size of farms in the United States had decreased "from 153 acres in 1870 to 134 acres in 1880." But George said that it was an "incontestable fact . . . that, like everything else, ownership of land is concentrating, and farming is assuming a larger scale." He also said that the census statement "that the average size of farms is decreasing in the United States" was "inconsistent not only with facts obvious all over the United States, and with the tendencies of agriculture in other countries, such as Great Britain, but it is inconsistent with the returns furnished by the Census Bureau itself" (40-41).

George's corrections were not taken lightly, and a wordy exchange resulted because he had called into question the intelligence and integrity of the interpreters who had failed to make sense out of their own census figures. He was proven to be correct in his criticism, however. Walker had misinterpreted the tables for 1870 and 1880 because he had assumed mistakenly that both sets of statistics were tabulated on the same principle. It turned out that the 1870 tables were based on improved land and the 1880 tables on total land. Walker's careless error had led him to compare sets of statistics that could not possibly be compared. The New York *Sun* summed up the long controversy, which amounted to about twenty-five pages and in which Walker had become rather contemptuous of George, by saying: "It is amusing because, while there is no lack of suavity and decorum on the part of Mr. George, his opponent squirms and sputters as one flagrant blunder after another is brought forward and the spike of logic is driven home through his egregious fallacies."[2] Walker's ironic offer to supply "a more elementary statement, illustrated with diagrams, if desired" had backfired.

Walker's criticism of George, like Sumner's, carried over to the *Princeton Review* and finally into a book, *Land and Its Rent*, in which a chapter was entitled, "Henry George's Social Fallacies." Though the academic critics had tried to ignore George, they could not. Much more slowly than their British counterparts, American economists had to come to some terms with him. That he had at least to be refuted was the common reaction, but he could not be ignored. In the years that were to come, hostile recognition and grudging acknowledgment of isolated ideas were as close as he came to academic acceptance. His earlier experiences at Berkeley had been an accurate forecast of his relations with orthodox and university political economists.

In *Social Problems*, George proved himself to be a keen logician, but his effectiveness can be traced in a large part to his skill as a writer, a skill that expressed his own personal zeal and the direction and inclinations of the "popular" American point of view:

> "Master"! We don't like the word. It is not American! But what is the use of objecting to the word when we have the thing? The man who gives me employment, which I must have or suffer, that man is my master, let me call him what I will. (48)

In turning men into machines we are wasting the highest powers. Already in our society there is a favored class who need take no thought for the morrow—what they shall eat, or what they shall drink, or wherewithal they shall be clothed. And may it be that Christ was more than a dreamer when he told his disciples that in that kingdom of justice for which he taught them to work and pray this might be the condition of all? (80)

And the same inequality of conditions which we see beginning here, is it not due to the same primary cause? American citizenship confers no right to American soil. The first and most essential rights of man—the rights to life, liberty and the pursuit of happiness—are denied here as completely as in England. And the same results must follow. (104)

The viewpoint of *Progress and Poverty* and of George's Christian socialism is once again in evidence:

By making land private property, by permitting individuals to appropriate this fund which nature plainly intended for the use of all, we throw the children's bread to the dogs of Greed and Lust; we produce a primary inequality which gives rise in every direction to other tendencies to inequality; and from this perversion of the good gifts of the Creator, from this ignoring and defying of his social laws, there arise in the very heart of our civilization those horrible and monstrous things that betoken social putrefaction. (218)

In our mad scramble to get on top of one another, how little do we take of the good things that bountiful nature offers us! Consider this fact: To the majority of people in such countries as England, and even largely in the United States, fruit is a luxury. Yet mother earth is not niggard of her fruit. If we chose to have it so, every road might be lined with fruit-trees. (240)

The beginning of 1884 found George back in England preaching that the promised land was promised to all.

II *Ireland and England (1881-82)*

George left the United States for England in October, 1881, as a special correspondent for the *Irish World.* Just a few days before his departure, Parnell and two other Irish members of Parliament had been jailed, increasing the already large number of political imprisonments. The unrest in Ireland made both

George and his books timely visitors to the British Isles. *Progress and Poverty* and *The Irish Land Question* were selling well throughout England, Scotland, and Ireland; and by early 1882 Kegan Paul had brought out a sixpenny and a threepenny edition of each book. Furthermore, free copies of each work were distributed to every member of Parliament and to various organizations and newspapers having any interest in practical approaches to economic problems.

While George was on his way, Parnell and his fellow prisoners composed their "No Rent Manifesto" which the *Irish World* published with praise and gusto. In one of George's first reports to the paper, he wrote as follows:

> It is not merely a despotism; it is a despotism sustained by alien force, and wielded in the interests of a privileged class, who look upon the great masses of the people as intended but to be hewers of their wood and drawers of their water. . . .
> I leave out of consideration for the moment the present extraordinary condition of things when constitutional guarantees for personal liberty are utterly suspended, and any man in the country may be hauled off to prison at the nod of an irresponsible dictator. I speak of the normal times and the ordinary workings of government.[3]

In a private letter, dated November 10th, to Patrick Ford, the editor of the *Irish World,* he said that "This is the most damnable government that exists to-day outside of Russia—Miss Taylor says outside of Turkey."[4] He finally was permitted a short visit with Parnell in Kilmainham jail. Speaking in public with great success on one occasion, he made his sympathies with the plight of the Irish unquestionably clear. He spent much of his time traveling about Ireland and witnessing the miserable conditions throughout the country, which he dutifully reported to the *Irish World.* By the first of the year (1882), he had concluded that "The majority of the Irish don't know yet how to get what they want. Like all great movements, it is a blind groping forward. But it is the beginning of the revolution, sure."[5]

Though George felt that the majority of the clergy was not on the side of the struggle for freedom in which the Irish were involved, he met some who greeted him warmly and who encouraged the movement in every way, including the Bishop of Clonfert; another bishop, Dr. Thomas Nulty; and Reverend

Thomas Dawson. He also formed a close friendship with the stepdaughter of John Stuart Mill, Helen Taylor, whom he considered to be the most intelligent woman he had ever met. With most of the men in jail, the women of the Irish Land Movement had become very active, and Miss Taylor had been a vital force among them.

In January, George returned to London and with his wife and daughters spent several weeks at Helen Taylor's home. Though Mrs. George and their daughters had come to England with him, he had gone to Ireland by himself. It was at this time that George met in person Henry Hyndman and Herbert Spencer, even spending some weeks in Hyndman's home.

George's meeting with Spencer was the beginning of their mutual antagonism. On the basis of his reading of *Social Statics,* George had expected Spencer to be sympathetic to the Irish cause. However, he was violently opposed to the Irish Land League and its ideas. Rent, Spencer thought, was rightfully due the landlord. George, of course, did not believe in "No Rent"— he wanted to confiscate it. The rift between the two proved to be as permanent as it was fundamental.

George's relations with Hyndman were amicable, but also basically at odds. Hyndman, an associate of William Morris in the Social Democratic Federation and the author of the socialistic *England for All,* was a Marxist. Personal animosity played no part in the ever-widening gulf between George and the true British left. Though their differences were there from the beginning, it was only after 1885-86 that the break became absolute.[6] The Marxists could never accept his defense of interest for one thing, and he could never accept the fundamental anti-individualism of socialist philosophy.

It was also during his winter visit in 1882 to London that George first met Joseph Chamberlain, a member of Gladstone's cabinet, who was in future years to be associated with radical programs for land-taxation legislation before passing from active political life. George was furiously busy into the early spring. And going back and forth between Ireland and London, he even managed a trip to Paris to see the Irish Land League leaders who were in exile.

During his year in England and on the Continent, George found he was always running out of time in which to get things

done. There were, however, three experiences or events of outstanding importance that occurred in 1882. The first was his influence upon Alfred Russel Wallace; the second, his reactions to
Parnell and the Phoenix Park murders and his arrests in Ireland
as a "suspicious" person; and, third, his effect (unknown to him)
upon a young and eventually famous playwright.

In the spring of 1882 George made contact with the active
Land Nationalist movement in England, headed by Wallace, the
eminent and respected associate of Darwin. Wallace admired
Progress and Poverty and even tried to interest Darwin in it. He
also sought George's help in order to get New York newspapers
to review his own book, *Land Nationalization*, a book clearly in
debt to *Progress and Poverty*. It not only quoted George frequently, often at length, but it also contained a chapter entitled
"Low Wages and Pauperism the Direct Consequences of Un-
restricted Private Property in Land," which indicated Wallace's
general agreement with George's program and ideas. Wallace's
support of George gave the author of *Progress and Poverty* the
kind of intellectual respectability he had never received in the
United States. The *Fortnightly Review* invited him to write an
article on Ireland, and it turned out to be as strong an attack
and as deft an analysis of the situation as he was ever to write.
Written in his best journalistic style, it appeared just a month
after the Phoenix Park murders. Having actually written it before the murders, George's words were all the more effective.
With devastating logic George traced the unrest in Ireland to
landlordism. Against the background of his analysis, the Phoenix
Park violence appeared inevitable.

With his *Fortnightly* article in the press,[7] George went to
Portland prison to meet Davitt, upon his release, on the very day
of the murders and therefore was not in Dublin. Davitt, whom
George had met in New York and who had been in jail from
before George's departure for Ireland the previous fall, had
always been more sympathetic to George's program than any of
the other Irish leaders. In *The Irish Land Question*, he had referred to Davitt's imprisonment and had also censured the
Parnellite policy: "Davitt is snatched to prison; a 'Liberal' government carries coercion by a tremendous majority, and the most
despotic powers are invoked to make possible the eviction of
Irish peasants. . . . It is already beginning to be perceived that

the Irish movement, so far as it has yet gone, is merely in the interest of a class; that, so far as it has yet voiced any demand, it promises nothing to the laboring and artisan classes" (98; 59). When Parnell had come to terms with the Gladstone government almost on the eve of the murders, Davitt and a great many of the disappointed Land Leaguers found themselves more than ever sympathetic to George's ideas. Between Parnell's "surrender" and the unfortunate and destructive assassinations, the Irish Land League had reached its unproductive end. In George's report to the *Irish World*, he recorded Davitt's and his own reaction to the disastrous and completely unnecessary violence:

> We [George and Davitt] did meet, but earlier than either he or I expected. I was awakened early in the morning by a telegram from a friend in Dublin, telling me that the new Chief Secretary and the Under-Secretary had been stabbed to death in Phoenix Park. But for the terms of the dispatch and the character of my friend I should have thought the story a wild rumor, for Dublin is a good place for rumors. But these left no doubt . . . I went at once to Davitt's room, woke him up, and handed him the dispatch as he lay in bed. "My God!" was his exclamation, "Have I got out of Portland to hear this!" And then he added mournfully: "For the first time in my life I despair. It seems like the curse that had always followed Ireland."[8]

Before returning to Ireland, George helped Parnell, Dillon, and Davitt put together a statement which the three signed, disassociating themselves and the movement from the murders. However, the Land League was dead, and Parnell turned his back upon it. George wrote to Ford on May 17th: "The whole situation is very bad and perplexing. The Land League in its present form on both sides of the water seems to me smashed. But the seed has at least been planted. . . . We who have seen the light must win because much greater forces than ourselves are working with us."[9]

George's usual transcendental confidence and optimism soothed him, but it did not blind him. "Parnell seems to me," he wrote again to Ford several days later (May 20th), "to have thrown away the greatest opportunity any Irishman ever had. It is the birthright for the mess of pottage."[10]

During the summer George set off in the company of James Leigh Joynes, a master of Eton College, in order to make a report to the *Irish World* on the state of affairs in western Ireland. Joynes was to report to the London *Times*. When they arrived in Loughrea, they were arrested almost immediately as "suspicious" strangers. George described the event with great wit: "The whole thing struck me as infinitely ridiculous. There was, after all, a good deal of human nature in Artemus Ward's declaration that he was willing to sacrifice all his wife's relatives to save the Union. And in my satisfaction in seeing an Eton master lugged through the town as too suspicious a stranger to be left at large I lost all sense of annoyance at my own arrest. In fact, my only regret was that it was not Kegan Paul."[11]

After being held for several hours, George and Joynes were released, and they left for Athenry a few miles away. Once there, George was arrested again, just as he and Joynes were boarding the train for Galway. Brought before the same magistrate, he was once again discharged: "The magistrate then summed up with a justification of the police for arresting me, and to my surprise finished by discharging me. Whether what had seemed to me the manifest purpose to require bail had been altered by the telegrams which Mr. Trevelyan stated in the House of Commons he had sent to Ireland on the subject, or whether it was the magistrate's own sense, I cannot tell."[12] The two arrests in three days under the Crimes Act enabled George to see, as he said, "the inside of two 'British Bastiles.'" It also gave him fine material to dispatch to the *Irish World*. Upon his release he handed out copies of *The Irish Land Question* to the magistrate and arresting officials.

Needless to say, the arrest of an American citizen as prominent as George made international news. James Russell Lowell, then United States minister, acted swiftly on his own by writing directly to Ireland to protest the arrest. George, however, made the most of the situation and wrote to President Arthur from Dublin on August 26th, saying in part, "that it is due to their own dignity that the United States should claim for their citizens travelling in countries with which they maintain relations of amity exemption from wanton annoyances, unreasonable inquisitions and imprisonment upon frivolous pretexts."[13] Apologies came in answer to both protests. Lowell was assured by Trevelyan, the secretary for Ireland, that George would not be in danger of the law. Eventually George himself received an apology from the British Foreign Office by way of Washington (October 17, 1882) on behalf of Her Majesty's Government.

George's year in the United Kingdom closed on a high note. After having publicized his books and after having seen to it that they would be widely distributed and influential through Kegan Paul's six- and threepenny editions, he found himself speaking in London in Memorial Hall in September to the Land Nationalist Society (George also spoke later in the month to a meeting of Church of England clergymen.) The meeting was presided over by Alfred Russel Wallace, who had tendered the invitation and who considered *Progress and Poverty* to be "undoubtedly the most remarkable and important work of the nineteenth century." At this time the London *Times* gave him its full attention by first publishing his letter (in which he had defended Joynes' participation in the Irish arrests and Joynes' views on Ireland which the *Times* had taken exception to), by commenting editorially, and finally by reviewing *Progress and Poverty* and *The Irish Land Question*. Also, it was at the Land Nationalist meeting at Memorial Hall that Bernard Shaw was converted to the cause for social reform. Shaw himself relates his experience:

> The result of my hearing that speech, and buying from one of the stewards of the meeting a copy of Progress & Poverty for sixpence (Heaven only knows where I got that sixpence) was that I plunged into a course of economic study, and at a very early stage of it became a Socialist and spoke from that very platform on the same great subject, and from hundreds of others as well . . . And that all the work was not mere gas, let the feats and pamphlets of the Fabian Society attest!
>
> When I was thus swept into the great Socialist revival of 1883, I found that five-sixths of those who were swept in with me had been converted by Henry George.[14]

George returned home in October to lecture and to involve himself in the series of articles in *Leslie's* that led to the quarrel with General Walker over the statistics and conclusions accompanying the 1880 United States Census and to the composition of *Social Problems*. Fourteen months later, the "apostle of plunder," as the hostile press called George, was back in England to preach self-evident truths with Emersonian eloquence. George had left the British Isles with many cordial invitations to return, including one from Professor Max Müller, the world famous Oxford scholar of Oriental literature and religion. At the invitation of the new Land Reform Union, he sailed for England for a second time in December of 1883. He had "hitched [his] wagon to a star," as he had suggested the Irish do when he had quoted the sage of Concord in *The Irish Land Question*. He had decided to act upon his own conclusion: "Both England and Scotland are ripe for . . . agitation, and, once fairly begun, it can have but one result—the victory of the popular cause" (63).

III   *Scotland and England (1883-85)*

"In speaking with special reference to the case of Ireland," George had written at the beginning of Chapter XII of *The Irish Land Question*, "I have, so far as general principles are concerned, been using it as a stalking-horse. In discussing the Irish Land Question, we really discuss the most vital of American questions" (73). These questions were apparently Scottish and English questions also. For "a little island or a little world," the remedy was the same—"make land common property."

Henry George's eldest son, who made the second trip to England in his company, says that "next to Gladstone," his father at the time was "the most talked of man in England."[15] There can be no doubt that George was a storm center, and that battle lines were forming. While George was at home, the opposition was consolidating in such movements as the "Property Defense League"; and lectures were being delivered by eminent men, such as Arnold Toynbee, to refute him. Articles of all sorts were written in order to counteract his ever-growing influence. Once the London *Times* had treated George as a serious threat to the established order, little time was lost by those who shared the paper's uneasiness. But George had the support of Helen Taylor, the Anglican clergyman Stewart Headlam, and the Unitarian Philip Wicksteed; and he also had the sympathy of journalists and publishers like William Saunders, James Durant, and William Reeves as well as young men like Sidney Oliver, a future Fabian and Secretary of State for India in Ramsay MacDonald's first Labor government forty or so years later. He even had the support of several prominent men of wealth, such as Thomas Briggs and Thomas Walker, just as he had had the support several years earlier of Francis Shaw—a fact that had surprised Shaw's in-law James Russell Lowell at the time of the Irish arrests. George was, indeed, the chief topic of conversation of anybody interested in economic questions, whether they were for or against him, or merely impartial students of current social problems.

When George arrived in Liverpool on New Year's Eve, he was met by Davitt and Richard McGhee, a Glasgow member of Parliament and one of his most ardent Scottish supporters. The next four months proved to be intensely active. Arrangements had been made for George to speak in the most important towns and cities of England. And George began his lecture schedule in London at a large meeting in St. James' Hall on January 9th, just a few months, interestingly enough, after Karl Marx's death in the same city. John Ruskin, who thought *Progress and Poverty* "an admirable book," had been asked to preside, but his ill health and age forced him to retire regretfully. He wished George "all success in his efforts, and an understanding audience."[16] Introduced as "George the Fifth," a title swiftly adopted by the press, his campaign was off to a roaring start. The next day almost every paper in the United Kingdom reported and commented upon his address and the packed house.

Social Problems was available in various editions and was selling well by the time George set forth on his tour. And sales of *Progress and Poverty*, according to one estimate, had reached nearly a hundred thousand copies. His previous visit, the publicity of his Irish arrests, and the reviews in most of the leading periodicals throughout 1883, which followed the review in the *Times* in the fall of 1882, had all contributed to his notoriety. After his London address, George himself realized how famous he had become. The intense and widespread response of the press—as hostile as it generally was—was ample proof. He wrote to his wife, "I can't begin to send you the papers in which I am discussed, attacked, and commented on—for I would have to send all the English, Scotch, and Irish papers. I am getting advertised to my heart's content and I shall have crowds wherever I go. . . ."[17]

Repeating his main ideas over and over again, George spoke effectively and without notes by adapting his speeches to the attitudes he sensed in each crowd that he addressed. After London, he went south and west to Plymouth, Cardiff, and Bristol, and from there north to Birmingham and into the Midlands. Organized opposition at speeches began to appear. His confiscationist program was beginning to gall moderates as much as it did conservatives. Even some of the Land Reform groups began to balk. The Liverpool *Post* editorialized on this point the day after his address in that city: "Mr. George's lecture in Liverpool last night had all the sweet and seductive beauty which has stolen away the judgment of many a reader of his famous book. . . . He apparently has convinced a large number of persons that thieving is no theft, for his great audience last night pronounced unanimously in favour of appropriating the land of the country and giving the present owners no compensation."[18] The crowd responded in spite of considerable opposition from local groups.

In February, George moved farther north into Scotland. With great success he repeated the "Moses" address on several occasions. He spoke in small towns, in the Highlands and in the Lowlands, and finally in Edinburgh and Glasgow. Scotland had proved George correct in his contention of two years before: it was riper for reform than either England or Ireland, especially for his nonconformist American variety.

George's effect in Scotland was very great and led to the formation of the Scottish Land Restoration League—Richard McGhee acting as one of the moving spirits and George writing a manifesto. Less than two months later, the English Land Restoration League was also organized. His powerful and permanent influence upon the labor movement in Scotland and the Scottish response to his religio-economic doctrines surpassed his lasting impact upon either the Irish or the English.

At the beginning of March, George returned to England and spoke in Leeds, Hull, Oxford, and Cambridge, finally returning to London. He spoke at Oxford University at Professor Max Müller's invitation; and when he finished his formal address, he asked for questions from his audience, as was often his practice. The meeting was turned into shambles by the eagerness of his listeners to turn the question period into a debate. The evening ended with George telling his audience that it was "the most disorderly meeting he had ever addressed."[19] Both he and Professor Müller were distressed, and apologies were made all around. Needless to say, George went on to Cambridge with much apprehension. Fortunately, he stayed in command of the situation there, and the meeting was quiet and orderly. George, however, was so exhausted from his three months of lecturing, that he went to see a doctor in London about his sleeplessness and his inability to relax sufficiently between engagements. But George finished his second visit to the British Isles by speaking a few more times in England and finally, at Davitt's invitation, in Dublin—his only Irish speech in the tour. On April 13th, he left from Queenstown for the United States, but by November of the same year he had returned for a third visit. He came alone this time.

George's third visit, at the invitation of the Land Restoration League, lasted a little less than three months, most of which was spent in Scotland. It did not seem that he had been away six months; and though this visit was shorter than the first two, it had been prepared for in the pages of *Nineteenth Century*. In the July number, George had replied to the Duke of Argyll's attack of the previous April. Now he had come to reap the fruit of the debate on the Duke's own ground. George's supporters had reprinted the two articles in cheap editions, and they had been well circulated. Everybody was apparently convinced that George had had the better of the exchange.

Again he began his campaign in St. James' Hall, London. From there his lecture tour took him almost immediately to Scotland where, after his initial address in Glasgow on November 21st, he spoke in about thirty different places, including Edinburgh. He finished the tour in London where he had begun it, but then he agreed to speak in Liverpool and Belfast where he was received by large enthusiastic crowds. The campaign had been generally successful, and "Moses" had again been very popular with Scottish audiences.

Unlike his previous campaign, publicity and newspaper coverage were relatively light. However, the visit did include a kind of double interview in the pages of *Nineteenth Century* in which both George and Hyndman presented their views on "Socialism and Rent Appropriation." Without sharing the moral philosophy of each other, each man praised the other for his war on poverty and for his desire to end the apathy and complacency that confronted social reform; but by then George's third visit was over. Elwood P. Lawrence sums up the character of George's second and third trips to the British Isles by stressing the major ideas that George himself emphasized:

> George's two objectives in his campaigns of 1884 and 1885 had been: first, to describe the evil living conditions of the workers of England and Scotland; and second, to prescribe the remedy. This twofold purpose was stated clearly in February 1884, in a circular addressed to the people of Scotland by the Scottish Land Restoration League. This circular contained the following argument: The Earth was created by God and therefore belonged to no one class or generation but to each generation; God intended the earth to be shared by his children, and every man, woman, and child derived from the Creator an equal right to the earth. (George, like Jefferson, assumed that there was a natural and divine law higher than the civil law.)
>
> Having established a basis for its authority, the circular proceeded to analyze conditions in Scotland. A denial of the equal right of all to the land was the primary cause of the current poverty and misery, and of their consequences: vice, crime, and degradation. The land of Scotland had been made the private property of a few persons; more than two thirds of the population were compelled to live in hovels, to work for starvation wages, and to subsist on insufficient food. George's speeches in 1884 and 1885 were, in part, a detailed elaboration of this theme.
>
> His analysis of British social problems was effective because it was simple, direct, and unprofessional. He described what he had seen—conditions with which his audiences were familiar; he named names and cited cases. His audiences were moved as much by his sincerity as by the facts he disclosed. British workers knew by bitter experience what their own conditions were; what they needed to know—and what George told them—was that poverty was *not* part of the natural order of things, that luxuries as well as necessities were due them by virtue of their labor, and that they must act to secure their just rewards.[20]

After he had returned home in February, 1885, George was asked to return to England to stand for Parliament. He replied: "I am at heart as much a citizen of Old England as of New England, but I think that from the accident of my birth I should be under disadvantage on your side of the water. At any rate, I should not deem it prudent to go over there, unless there was such a considerable call as made it seem clearly my duty."[21]

When the "soldier in the Liberative War of Humanity" had left England after his second visit, many ironic titles had been added to his name: the "apostle of plunder" had become also "George the Fifth," "Saint George," and finally the "Prophet of San Francisco." "M.P." was one title he was never to have. George was truly the prophet that the Duke of Argyll glibly dubbed him, and that is the major reason why he was never to be a professor of political economy or the mayor of New York City any more than he was ever to be a member of Parliament. His effect upon English radicalism and on labor and land movements remained that of a prophet, and both he and his supporters thought it, even then, a very fine and very apt title indeed. The Duke of Argyll was right about one thing at least.

IV   The Peer and The Prophet *and* Protection or Free Trade

George's debate with the Duke of Argyll and his book on the tariff question were the highlights of his writing career from 1884 to 1886. "The Prophet of San Francisco" appeared in the same month in which George left England after his second visit, reaching him on the eve of his departure. George, who had known the peer by reputation, had admired his book *The Reign of Law*; but he also knew of Argyll's support of the landlords in Ireland and his opposition to the liberalizing of Irish land laws. When George's supporters in the Scottish Land Restoration League urged him to answer the attack, he agreed because Argyll was a worthy opponent and because he represented all that George had been speaking against in Ireland, England, and Scotland. George began immediately writing "The 'Reduction to Iniquity,'" but he finally decided to take his manuscript with him to New York in order to "polish it like a steel shot."

Even using the fact that he was once a recipient of a complimentary copy of *Progress and Poverty* from the author, the Duke of Argyll was consistently ironic throughout his article. Though witty and condescending, it was an effectively argued article. There could be no mistake about its meaning: George was a Communist, a pessimist, and hopelessly lost in self-contradiction. Including both *Progress and Poverty* and *Social Problems* in his survey of George's ideas, the Duke felt it "not a little remarkable to find one of the most extreme doctrines of Communism advocated by a man who is a citizen of the United States." He said George based much of his argument on surplus population but rejected Malthus. He said George had also contradicted himself by speaking about the corruption of democracy on one hand while urging redistribution of wealth and land on the other hand. In his concluding paragraph, the Duke said that in "mathematical reasoning the 'reduction to absurdity' is one of the most familiar methods of disproof. In political reasoning the 'reduction to iniquity' ought to be of equal value." He wrote that George's "erroneous data" had overpowered his "Moral Sense." "The Prophet of San Francisco" was certainly a well-written presentation for landlordism and a hierarchial society. Argyll even used the Bible in a Georgian manner, thus parodying his opponent's style:

> In olden times, under violent and rapacious rulers, the Prophets of Israel and of Judah used to raise their voices against all forms of wrong and robbery, and they pronounced a special benediction upon him who sweareth to his own hurt and changeth not. But the new Prophet of San Francisco is of a different opinion. Ahab would have been saved all his trouble, and Jezebel would have been saved all her tortuous intrigues if only they could have had beside them the voice of Mr. Henry George. Elijah was a fool. What right could Naboth have to talk about the "inheritance of his fathers"? His fathers could have no more right to acquire the ownership of those acres on the Hill of Jezreel than he could have to continue in the usurpation of it. No matter what might be his pretended title, no man and no body of men could give it:—not Joshua nor the Judges; not Saul nor David; not Solomon in all his glory—could "make sure" to Naboth's fathers that portion of God's earth against the undying claims of the head of the State, and of the representative of the whole people of Israel. (22-23)

George, he said, had promulgated ideas that would "abolish the Decalogue" and had "forgotten—strangely forgotten—some of the most fundamental facts of Nature."

George chose Argyll's own words for the title of his reply, a reply that was equal to Argyll's in wit, rhetoric, and logic, and which received no rejoinder from the peer—even after the Scottish Land Restoration League and other radical groups had reprinted the two articles in pamphlet form under the titles *The Peer and the Prophet* or *Property in Land* and had circulated it throughout Scotland as if it were the Declaration of Independence. (The pamphlet appeared in several editions throughout the British Isles.) "The 'Reduction to Iniquity'" contradicted Argyll's contention that the landlords improved the land or the community and increased capital. He described Scotland accurately and boldly. He compared the slavery of the Scot to that of the Negro in the Southern United States and pointed out how the conditions in Scotland were even worse. The most brutal Southern American slaveholder would not have interfered with a Negro slave's religion, which was more than could be said of a Scottish landlord. He used the Isle of Skye to demonstrate the extent of Scottish poverty and to show that overpopulation had nothing to do with it; the curse upon Scotland was landlordism. He made his usual American declaration for equality and human rights, saying that the duke and the peasant were in body and spirit the same and, were they to change places, would be indistinguishable. His comments had the ring of Mark Twain's *The Prince and the Pauper* and anticipated the spirit of *Pudd'nhead Wilson*, for George wrote:

> Place, stripped of clothes, a landowner's baby among a dozen workhouse babies, and who that you call in can tell the one from the others? Is the human law which declares the one born to the possession of a hundred thousand acres of land, while the others have no right to a single square inch, conformable to the intent of Nature or not? Is it, judged by this appeal, natural or unnatural, wise or foolish, righteous or iniquitous? Put the bodies of a duke and a peasant on a dissecting-table, and bring, if you can, the surgeon who, by laying bare the brain or examining the viscera, can tell which is duke and which is peasant? (52)

Some of George's paragraphs in "The 'Reduction to Iniquity'" are his fiery best and give the reader a very good idea of why he was so effective in his speeches in the British Isles during his first three tours:

> But to return to the "reduction to iniquity." Test the institution of private property in land by its fruits in any country where it exists. Take Scotland. What, there, are its results? That wild beasts have supplanted human beings; that glens which once sent forth their thousand fighting men are now tenanted by a couple of gamekeepers; that there is destitution and degradation that would shame savages; that little children are stunted and starved for want of proper nourishment; that women are compelled to do the work of animals; that young girls who ought to

be fitting themselves for wifehood and motherhood are held to the monotonous toil of factories, while others, whose fate is sadder still, prowl the streets; that while a few Scotsmen have castles and palaces, more than a third of Scottish families live in one room each, and more than two-thirds in not more than two rooms each; that thousands of acres are kept as playgrounds for strangers, while the masses have not enough of their native soil to grow a flower, are shut out even from moor and mountain; dare not take a trout from a loch or a salmon from the sea! (59-60)

George's voice was clearly an American one:

If the Duke thinks all classes have gained by the advance in civilization, let him go into the huts of the Highlands. There he may find countrymen of his, men and women the equals in natural ability and in moral character of any peer or peeress. . . . These human beings are in natural parts and powers just such human beings as may be met at a royal levee, at a gathering of scientists, or inventors, or captains of industry. That they so live and work, is not because of their stupidity, but because of their poverty—the direct and indisputable result of the denial of their natural rights. (60-61)

The Scottish people, George said, were prevented from participating in the general advance of civilization and were, in fact, worse off than their ancestors, "They have been driven from the good land to the poor land." Let the Duke of Argyll "apply the 'reduction of iniquity'" to the facts, George repeated as he catalogued the grievances that he said could be justly held against the landowners of Scotland. "I hold with Thomas Jefferson, that 'the earth belongs in usufruct to the living, and that the dead have no power or right over it'" (48). He even invoked the "American Indian Chief, Black Hawk" for having declared the "first and universal perception of mankind" when he said that "'The Great Spirit has told me that land is not to be made property like other property. The earth is our mother!'" (50).

George concluded by saying that the manifesto of the Scottish Land Restoration League, which called upon the Scottish people to "bind themselves together" in order to free themselves of landlordism, was "a lark's note in the dawn." Scotland, like Ireland or England, was not an isolated case—"everywhere the same spirit is rising, the same truth is beginning to force its way."

George's supporters eagerly proclaimed his ideas and invited him to come to Argyll's own countryside in order to beard the laird in his lair. George reluctantly interrupted his work upon *Protection or Free Trade* and went to the British Isles for his third successful campaign to spread his gospel.

George had been planning *Protection or Free Trade* for several years, for it was to be in some ways the capitalistic companion of the socialistic *Social Problems*. Both books had their genesis in George's opposition to monopoly, whether in industry or in land. He had made an abortive start on the tariff book between his first and second visits to the British Isles (work on it had been interrupted and the manuscript had been lost), and now that he had replied to the Duke of Argyll he was able to give his complete attention to it. However, he was again interrupted; he was not able to complete it until after his return from his third trip to Britain, the speaking tour of Scotland in 1884-85. Having sporadically thus engaged himself in a manner of composition very different from the intense period that saw the creation of *Progress and Poverty*, George was actually fortunate to have finished *Protection or Free Trade* before his first mayoralty campaign which began in the late summer of 1886.

The subtitle of *Protection or Free Trade* says it is *An Examination of the Tariff Question, with especial regard to the Interests of Labor*. In his preface George said that he aimed "to determine whether protection or free trade better accords with the interests of labor, and to bring to a common conclusion on this subject those who really desire to raise wages." He took thirty chapters in which to make his case, some of which had appeared in article form before the book was finished. *Protection or Free Trade* was published in 1886 by Henry George and Company (consisting of George and his second son, Richard), but it had been serialized in newspapers in the last half of the previous year.

Protection or Free Trade is an aggressively anti-protectionist book. At one point George imagines a conversation between a protectionist and his favorite character, Robinson Crusoe:

Let us suppose an American protectionist is the first to break his solitude with the long yearned-for music of human speech. Crusoe's delight we can well imagine. . . . Let us suppose that after having heard Crusoe's story, . . . our protectionist prepares to depart, but before going seeks to offer some kindly warning of the danger Crusoe will be exposed to from the "deluge of cheap goods" that passing ships will seek to exchange for fruit and goats. Imagine him to tell Crusoe just what protectionists tell larger communities, . . . that, unless he takes measures to make it difficult to bring these goods ashore, his industry will be entirely ruined. . . . Are these arguments for protection a whit more absurd when addressed to one man living on an island than when addressed to sixty millions living on a continent? What would be true in the case of Robinson Crusoe is true in the case of Brother Jonathan. If foreigners will bring us goods cheaper than we can make them ourselves, we shall be the gainers. The more we get in imports as compared with what we have to give in exports, the better the trade for us. And since foreigners are not liberal enough to give us their productions, but will only let us have them in return for our own productions, how can they ruin our industry? The only way they could ruin our industry would be by bringing us for nothing all we want, so as to save us the necessity for work. (113-15)

The effectiveness of George's style is readily apparent. It is readable and amusing.

Protection or Free Trade is, however, a frankly pro-capitalistic book, and it emphasizes the very things which caused the doctrinaire Socialists and Marxists in Europe to become impatient and finally disenchanted with George. After quoting a protectionist economist, Professor R. E. Thompson, on Charles Fourier, George attacks Fourier's reasoning as harshly as he does Thompson's elsewhere in the book. His comments are a defense of the "middlemen":

This story, quoted approvingly to convey an idea that the trader is a mere toll-gatherer, simply shows what a superficial thinker Fourier was. If he had undertaken to bring with him to Paris a supply of apples and to carry them around with him so that he could have one when he felt like it he would have formed a much truer idea of what he was really paying for in the increased price. That price included not merely the cost of the apple at its place of growth, plus the cost of transporting it to Paris, . . . the loss of damaged apples, and remuneration for the service and capital of the wholesaler, who held the apples in stock until the vender chose to take them, but also payment to the vender, for standing all day in the streets of Paris, in order to supply a few apples to those who wanted an apple *then* and *there*. (64-65)

George tries once again, as he did in *Progress and Poverty* and *Social Problems*, to make clear his uneasiness with the word "socialism":

> Let us endeavor, as well as can in brief be done, to trace the relations between the conclusion to which we have come and what, with various shades of meaning, is termed "socialism."
>
> The term "socialism" is used so loosely that it is hard to attach to it a definite meaning. I myself am classed as a socialist by those who denounce socialism, while those who profess themselves socialists declare me not to be one. For my own part I neither claim nor repudiate the name, and realizing as I do the correlative truth of both principles can no more call myself an individualist or a socialist than one who considers the forces by which the planets are held to their orbits could call himself a centrifugalist or a centripetalist. The German socialism of the school of Marx (of which the leading representative in England is Mr. H. M. Hyndman, and the best exposition in America has been given by Mr. Laurence Gronlund) seems to me a high-purposed but incoherent mixture of truth and fallacy, the defects of which may be summed up in its want of radicalism—that is to say, of going to the root. (302-3)

Nevertheless, he uses the word and tries to bridge another paradox in two key paragraphs near the end of the book. They reflect that dichotomy on which *Progress and Poverty* and all of George's works are based.

> Individualism and socialism are in truth not antagonistic but correlative. Where the domain of the one principle ends that of the other begins. And although the motto *Laissez faire* has been taken as the watchword of an individualism that tends to anarchism, and so-called free traders have made "the law of supply and demand" a stench in the nostrils of men alive to social injustice, there is in free trade nothing that conflicts with a rational socialism. On the contrary, we have but to carry out the free-trade principle to its logical conclusions to see that it brings us to such socialism.
>
> The free-trade principle is, as we have seen, the principle of free production—it requires not merely the abolition of protective tariffs, but the removal of all restrictions upon production. (308)

True, *laissez faire* meant that land values had also to be appropriated because free trade and free production meant the end of all private monopoly of land. "True free trade," he said, "requires that the active factor of production, Labor, shall have free access to the passive factor of production, Land. To secure this all monopoly of land must be broken up, and the equal right of all to the use of the natural elements must be secured by the treatment of the land as the common property in usufruct of the whole people" (289). It was a point to which even the aged and ill Whitman responded favorably.

George is a socialist in a united world where the many nationalistic states must become like the states in the American Union. In fact, "Common Market" reasoning dominates *Protection or Free Trade.* Individualistic and socialistic motives need no more be at odds than economic progress and social amelioration, or political evolution and moral growth. Protection, he says, is "repugnant to moral perceptions and inconsistent with the simplicity and harmony which we everywhere discover in natural law"—a very Whitmanian, Thoreauvian, and Emersonian contention.

So far as George was concerned, land taxation and free trade went together. It was not necessary to be a protectionist if one was pro-labor, for high tariffs were a false security that only closed down markets, lessened trade, and stultified production by eliminating the need to produce. In the end, labor suffered because jobs became scarce as production decreased; production fell off as need lessened; and need remained unfulfilled because labor was unemployed and therefore without the capital to satisfy its needs. The results were want and poverty amid plenty, or potential plenty. Trading freely, each part of the world would help the other and be helped in return, thereby contributing to the general good of all and to the general advance of civilization. George would not have shared Thoreau's belief that the curse of trade even effects man's bargains with heaven, but he might well have understood why Thoreau thought so. After all, George might have said, trade is as different from the love of trade as money is from the love of money. Cooperation means that more than one must operate, which Thoreau well knew.

Protection or Free Trade sold about two hundred thousand copies in the five years or so that followed its publication, and it was almost immediately translated into several languages. Its actual popularity and influence in George's lifetime, however, were uneven. There was no English edition until 1903, six years after the author's death. Nevertheless, George had the unique experience of seeing his book printed in the *Congressional Record* in its entirety in 1892 when six members of the House of Representatives, led by Tom Johnson of Ohio, read it as part of the tariff debate. Needless to say, George was delighted, for more than a million copies were run off and mailed everywhere that year in the United States, including the ten thousand that went to England.

However, the printing in the *Congressional Record* was really a part of the last ten years of George's life, most of which were spent in political activity. In 1886, George was just beginning his decade of campaigning and had yet to experience the pressure of practical politics. *Protection or Free Trade* stood on its own as the work of the author of *Progress and Poverty,* the man who had set the British Isles on fire with the desire for social reform. It was not the work of the candidate for mayor of New York City, but it almost coincided with his agreement to run under the auspices of New York labor unions. However, George's domestic political activity and his association with labor groups from 1885 to his death helped to circulate the book until *Protection or Free Trade,* with the help of the *Congressional Record,* was almost as widely distributed and in as great a number as *Progress and Poverty.*

Protection or Free Trade and George's political speeches were based upon fundamental ideas of long standing. He proclaimed them clearly in a speech, "The Crime of Poverty,"[22] which he made in Burlington, Iowa, on April 1, 1885, under the sponsorship of the local chapter of the Knights of Labor. The speech and George's sponsor indicated the direction in which George was headed as much as it betrayed the direction from which he had come:

> There is a cause for this poverty; and, if you trace it down, you will find its root in a primary injustice. Look over the world today—poverty everywhere. The cause must be a common one. You cannot attribute it to the tariff, or to the form of government, or to this thing or to that in which nations differ; because, as deep poverty is common to them all, the cause that produces it must be a common cause. What is that common cause? There is one sufficient cause that is common to all nations; and that is, the appropriation as the property of some, of that natural element on which, and from which, all must live.[23]

CHAPTER 5

The Philosopher-Politician:
The Struggle for More Than
Honor in His Own Land

I *George's Campaigns for Office and the* Standard, *1886-87*

IN 1886 George reached the peak of his career as a personal symbol of reform. He had become by then a respected writer with an international reputation. He had even won honors as an economist and social philosopher at home, but the scope of his political influence was not so great as it was in the British Isles. During the summer the opportunity came to participate actively in American politics as a candidate for office as well as a spokesman for a cause and a theory. The Central Labor Union of New York City asked George to run for mayor. As he said just after the election, he "was nominated because it was believed that [he] best represented the protest against unjust social conditions and the best means of remedying them."[1]

The Central Labor Union, whose own course of development ran roughly parallel to George's, had grown from a group of delegates from labor organizations that had been formed in the winter of 1881-82 at a mass meeting at Cooper Union, called to express the collective sympathy of New York workingmen for the downtrodden people of Ireland in their struggle with landlordism. It was almost a matter of course that the Central Labor Union should have turned to George in its effort to grasp political power, for by this time George's international commitment to labor and to the Irish had been well established. On receiving the invitation, he made one unusual condition before he would allow his name to be put forward in nomination: the

Union had to prove to him that the rank-and-file workingman was behind the idea by securing a petition with at least thirty thousand signatures. A month later it submitted to George the names of 34,460 voters who had pledged him their votes.[2]

In addition to his comment after the election about the reasons for his nomination, George had said in reply to the Central Labor Union's invitation that it seemed to him that a movement for labor reform should begin in "our municipalities, where we may address ourselves to what lies nearest at hand, and avoid dissensions that, until the process of economic education has gone further, might divide us on national issues. The foundation of our system is in our local governments."[3] The dissension came soon enough during the state-wide campaign the next year.

In September, George wrote to his old friend, Dr. E. R. Taylor, in San Francisco: "All the probabilities are that I will be in the fight, and it is by no means impossible that I will be elected. But the one thing sure is that if I do go in the campaign will bring the land question into practical politics and do more to popularise its discussion than years of writing could do. This is the only temptation to me."[4] Such was the reason a social philosopher must have in order to abandon his study for the hurly-burly of a political campaign. George was however, an agitator of long standing, and the choice was not a hard one. In his personal letter to Taylor, he was simply making it clear that desires or ambitions for personal glory had no part in his decision. On the basis of all the evidence, there is no reason whatever to question his motives nor his explanation. The campaign gave George opportunity to spread his gospel.

In his "Bunker Hill" address the night of the election, after most of the votes had been tabulated, he suggested that the fight had only begun and that the forces of labor had won a victory, despite having lost the immediate battle: "Thank God, we have made a beginning. We have demonstrated the political power of labor. Never again—never again, will the politicians look upon a labor movement with contempt."[5] George had hopes for a national labor party and thought that labor's rights would soon be affirmed. But New York City politics then, as now, was a thing apart. In November, 1886, he could never have believed the disastrous defeat of the next year. In cheering his disappointed supporters the night of the mayoralty election, the philosopher-politician believed what he said, "We have done in this campaign more for popular education, more to purify politics, more toward the emancipation of labor from individual slavery, than could have been accomplished in twenty years of ordinary agitation."[6] As public propaganda of the hour that much may well have been true. Its lasting effect upon practical politics, however, was another thing altogether.

The campaign had been brief but intense. Labor organizations rallied to the call, with Samuel Gompers chairing the city organization of Henry George clubs and running the speakers' bureau. At one point early in the campaign, the Democratic organization tried to get George to remove himself voluntarily from the contest. In a statement made just before his death and in the midst of his 1897 campaign, George said:

> Before my nomination had formally taken place I received a request from Mr. William M. Ivins, then Chamberlain of the city, and a close political friend and representative of Mr. Grace, to privately meet him. I did so at Seighortner's, on Lafayette Place. We sat down in a private room, unattended, and smoked some cigars together. Mr. Ivins insisted that I could not possibly be elected Mayor of New York, no matter how many people might vote for me; that the men who voted knew nothing of the real forces that dominated New York. He said that I could not possibly be counted in. He offered on behalf of Tammany Hall and the County Democracy that if I would refuse the nomination for mayor they would run me for Congress, select a city district in which the nomination of the two was equivalent to election; that I should be at no expense whatever, but might go to Europe or anywhere I willed, and when I came back should receive a certificate of election to the House of Representatives. I said to him finally: "You tell me I cannot possibly get the office. Why, if I cannot possibly get the office, do you want me to withdraw?" His reply was: "You cannot be elected, but your running will raise hell!" I said: "You have relieved me of embarrassment. I do not want the responsibility and the work of the office of the Mayor of New York, but I do want to raise hell! I am decided and will run."[7]

Judged by "hell-raising" standards, George's 1886 campaign was a magnificent and unqualified success. As the Democratic organization in the city had feared, the election results were as disquieting to the establishment as was the campaign publicity generated by labor before the election. Without the support of any of New York's major newspapers, labor's voice was confined mainly to a German paper and the *Leader*, the Central Labor Union's own hastily thrown together daily. Speaking up to a dozen times a day all over the city, George was joined by many of his supporters in round-the-clock speech-making. The final official results gave his opponent, Abram S. Hewitt, the Democratic candidate, 90,552 and the "third party" candidate, Theodore Roosevelt, the Republican nominee, 60,435. George polled 68,110. The election had been a struggle between George and Hewitt, independent labor and the Democratic machine. Roosevelt and the Republicans were never in the race. In fact, the "Red scare" and labor-anarchy opinions caused worried anti-socialist elements in the Republican Party to desert Roosevelt during the campaign in order to support Hewitt and were later assailed for their dishonesty by the future President. So far as Roosevelt was concerned, George was at least an honest man, something that could not be said of Tammany Hall and the Democratic machine.

The election showed clearly George's current popularity and labor's apparent strength in the city. Perhaps, George thought, its potential was even greater than the almost seventy thousand votes given him. A national party was a distinct possibility. In addition, George believed that in reality he had been elected and then "counted out," that Hewitt's twenty-two thousand vote margin of victory was the result of organizational tampering. In his "Bunker Hill" remarks, George said: "They may bribe, they may count us out, by their vile arts they may defeat what would be an honest verdict of the people; but we have gained what we fought for." "Under a fair vote of the people of New York," he went on to say, "I would be to-night elected Mayor."[8] Whether or not Tammany had been able to control the election by manipulating affairs at the district level and elsewhere remains a moot point. There were many, however, who shared and have continued to share George's opinion.[9]

Several permanent patterns for the future resulted from the election: (1) George's anti-poverty program and the single tax remedy were in politics for some time to come; (2) George and the Roman Catholic Church participated in a drawn-out private and public debate—and a strange dialogue it was; (3) George's

New York newspaper, the weekly *Standard*, was born, a fellow organ for a time of the United Labor Party's daily and campaign-founded *Leader*; and (4) labor political activity was intensified locally and nationally with the birth of the United Labor Party —a party which George for a time hoped would draw together all the workingmen of America in a single powerful and politically effective force for social reform.

On January 8, 1887, the first number of the *Standard* was published, appearing weekly until August, 1892. Its publication began when serious consideration was being given to George's chances for president in 1888, and two days after the convention of the United Labor party. During the summer the new party leaders called for a convention which was to be held in Syracuse on August 17th in order to prepare for state and municipal contests to be decided in November. For the moment at least, labor had gone several steps beyond the old Knights of Labor or even the Central Labor Union in its effort to assert political force and pressure. On the basis of its showing in George's mayoralty campaign, hopes were high that the strength of the labor movement would continue to grow, first in New York State in 1887 and then nationally in 1888. George's supporters, who shared his hopes for a united front, were soon disillusioned by the trouncing they received at the New York State polls that November.

Once again the fundamental ideological split between George's policies and those of the socialists became apparent. Some time before the convention met, the socialists in the party began to proclaim essential Marxist doctrine. They said "that the burning social question is not a land tax, but the *abolition of all private property in instruments of production.*"[10] This demand was one of the basic points of difference between George and the British socialists. George countered by writing that "either they must go out" of the party "or that the majority must go out, for it is certain that the majority of the men who constitute the united labor party do not propose to nationalize capital and are not in favor of the abolition of all private property in the 'instruments of production.'"[11] Though the *Leader*, in socialist hands, attacked George, he and his supporters had their way at the convention, and the socialists founded their own party. The split was permanent and irreparable.

After the election, George wrote to his friend, the German translator of *Progress and Poverty*, C. D. F. Gutschow, in San Francisco, explaining his course of action:

> I have no doubt whatever that the notion that I had turned on the socialists as a mere matter of policy was widely disseminated among our German population and did me harm, for this was the socialists' persistent cry through their German papers and I had no way of correcting it. The truth however is just the reverse. Beginning about January of this year [1887], they made the most persistent efforts to force socialistic doctrines upon us. I did not resist and refused even to enter into controversy with them until it became absolutely necessary. There was no alternative other than to consent to have the movement ranked as a socialistic movement or to split with the socialists. Although this lost us votes for the present I am perfectly certain that it will prove of advantage in the long run. Policy, however, did not enter into my calculations; I was only anxious to do the right thing.

It was characteristic of George to want "to do the right thing." His certainty about advantages "in the long run" stemmed, however, from his philosophical rather than from his practical grasp of political affairs. Discussing his position with regard to the convicted anarchists in the Chicago Haymarket Riot, a position which was bitterly attacked by many prominent British Socialists who had once supported him, like William Morris and Hyndman, George wrote in the same letter:

> Second, as to the Anarchists. . . . Our bench is not immaculate, but I could not believe that every one of seven men, with the responsibility of life and death hanging over him, could unjustly condemn these men. In spite of all pressure I refused to say anything about the matter until I had a chance to somewhat examine it for myself, and a reading of the decision of the Supreme Court convinced me, as it did everyone else whom I got to read it, that the men had not been condemned as I had previously supposed, for mere opinion and general utterances. . . .
>
> It is in the nature of things that the man who acts solely by conscience must often be misunderstood, and seem to others as if he were acting from low motives when in reality he is acting from the highest. This cannot be avoided, but I so much value your esteem and your friendship that I want to make this personal explanation to you.[12]

To be great and yet to be misunderstood is an axiomatic Emersonian truth, but George's position was one which Thoreau, the defender of John Brown, would not have taken no matter what company he accidentally kept. That George believed men could be as objective as he in the heat of ideological clashes or in cases where their interests may have been involved does credit to his abiding faith in the capacity of human beings to act justly under any circumstances—whatever it may say about his understanding of the ways in which climates of opinion are created. His faith in human reason would have made Jonathan Swift smile. Needless to say, George's break with the socialists also split the *Leader* and the *Standard* as fellow organs of labor opinion. Whatever may be said of the philosophical and theoretical differences, however, the cleavage between the socialists and George was unfortunate for the united forces of labor in the day-to-day battle for social reform.

Running at the head of the ticket for Secretary of State, George hoped for 150,000 votes. He was soundly beaten, receiving only 72,000. The Republican candidate totaled 459,000 and the Democratic winner 480,000. Within New York City itself, he polled barely one-half of the 68,000 he had received the year before. As a national party, United Labor had aborted. Though George was to run again for office in 1897, his mayoralty campaign of 1886 was his most successful attempt as a practical politician; it was the closest he was to come to holding elective office in his own land. George, however, was not a personally ambitious man. He had made it clear many times that "It was never 'my principles,' 'my movement,' 'my cause'; but always 'our principles,' 'our movement,' 'our cause.' "[13]

II *McGlynn, Catholic Churchmen, Pope Leo and the Anti-Poverty Society*

George's efforts in the last half of the decade that followed the publication of *Progress and Poverty* went mainly into his editorial labors on the *Standard*, much of which was concerned with the Catholic Church and its attitudes toward him, his political activity at home and abroad, his Catholic supporters, and the principles on which his major work was based.[14] One of the chief developments of the 1887 campaign which helped to defeat George was the open and powerful opposition of the Roman Catholic Church. As a result of this opposition, the *Irish World*, for which George had written his dispatches from Ireland and which had supported him in his race for mayor the year before, came out against him. George was therefore attacked by the church and the Irish-Catholic press on one hand, and by the socialists and socialist press, including the *Leader* and the *Volkzeitung* (the former pro-George, German language newspaper) on the other hand. The opposition of the church was roused by George's spirited defense of his supporter, Father Edward McGlynn of St. Stephen's, one of the largest churches in the city. George's attacks upon the Catholic Church for trying to silence McGlynn dominated many of the *Standard's* early issues during the first half of 1887.

McGlynn had met George for the first time late in 1882 after George's celebrated visit to Ireland and England. He had already read *Progress and Poverty* and had spoken publicly in support of George and George's crusade while the *Irish World* correspondent was still abroad. Sharing many views about labor and poverty, and also the cause of the Irish, the two men became intimate friends. Four years later, George in fact asked McGlynn his opinion about the race for mayor, and McGlynn advised him to accept the nomination and to run.

McGlynn came into general public notice at a meeting sponsored by the *Irish World* in the summer of 1882. It was called to organize support for Davitt who was once again in the United States after his release from Portland prison. Davitt, who had been accused of being "captured" by George, was asked to explain that he and the Land League had not lost their identities. In his public address McGlynn told Davitt to "preach the gospel" and not make excuses for it or explain it. In a rousing speech that was received with loud cheers, he said "that if I had to fall into the arms of anybody, I don't know a man into whose arms I should be more willing to fall than into the arms of Henry George."[15]

Five years later in 1887, he explained in the *Standard* his initial difficulties in speaking publicly on behalf of George: "I voluntarily promised to abstain from making land league speeches, not because I acknowledge the right of any one to

forbid me, but because I know too well the power of my ecclesiastical superiors to impair and almost destroy my usefulness in the ministry of Christ's Church to which I had consecrated my life."[16]

Despite the repeated warnings between 1882 and 1886, McGlynn publicly supported George in his campaigns in 1886 and 1887. Though already suspended and removed from his church by Archbishop Corrigan, McGlynn continued to spread George's ideas, delivering a strong address at the end of March, 1887, at the Academy of Music, entitled "The Cross of the New Crusade." Punctuated by cheers and applause from a largely Catholic audience, he said again there was no conflict between George's idea of the land for the people and the fundamental truths of the Church. More than any other event, this speech brought about the formation of the Anti-Poverty Society—the idea for the organization and its name having been originally suggested by a member of the *Standard*. McGlynn was named president and George vice-president. The first meeting of the society was held on May 1st in a packed hall from which thousands were turned away. The next Sunday evening, which with the previous Sunday established the normal meeting time, was a repetition of the first meeting. The only difference was that George rather than McGlynn gave the major address. Denounced and ridiculed by the press, the Anti-Poverty Society was for a time very popular and well-supported. Many papers, in fact, took advantage of McGlynn's difficulties with his superiors to snipe at both the labor movement and the Roman Catholic Church.

In 1887, McGlynn was threatened with excommunication and in May was given forty days in which to get to Rome. To George, events were unmistakable and the signs clear. In the *Standard's* last number for June, he compared McGlynn to Galileo.[17] George's choice of a historical analogy was not particularly precise, but it was effective. Galileo had been imprisoned, George demonstrated, for having asserted an obvious truth. McGlynn was being punished for stating the truth about land and labor, which, George implied, would some day be as obvious and as accurate as seeing "that the earth revolves around the sun." There "will arise by the spot" where McGlynn "shall be excommunicated" a statue and an inscription the like of those dedicated to Galileo; for McGlynn, "the true-hearted American priest," had seen, as had George himself, the fundamental economic facts and principles around which human poverty revolved.

McGlynn's discovery of these universal economic laws were not to be acknowledged, however; for after expressly refusing to go to Rome, he was finally excommunicated on July 3rd by Archbishop Corrigan. Henry George, Jr. tells us that the Archbishop did not stop at excommunication, but instead harassed McGlynn's sympathizers, clerical and lay, and even "In two instances . . . prevented burial of persons in the Catholic Calvary Cemetery, because, while these persons were known to be strict in their duties to the Church, they attended the Anti-Poverty Society lectures of Dr. McGlynn."[18] Perhaps Patrick Ford's action during the 1887 campaign, when the *Irish World* turned against the United Labor Party, should not have surprised McGlynn and George so completely as it did.

It was not until 1892 that the McGlynn case was finally closed. In 1891, Pope Leo had sent Archbishop Satolli to the United States to review the case of Father McGlynn, and a board of Catholic clerics who were also professors at the Catholic University in Washington examined the evidence. Dr. Burtsell and McGlynn submitted statements explaining once again the excommunicated priest's adherence to George's land tax principles. After McGlynn promised Archbishop Satolli that he would present himself to the Pope within four months, the bans of excommunication were lifted. Archbishop Corrigan, somewhat astonished by the entire procedure, sent Father McGlynn to a parish in Newburgh, New York, just north of New York City. According to Henry George, Jr., McGlynn "went to Rome some months afterwards and was accorded an interview by the Pope. The reference to the social question was of briefest description. 'Do you teach against private property?' asked his Holiness. 'I do not; I am staunch for private property,' said the Doctor. 'I thought so,' said his Holiness, and he conferred his blessing."[19]

Two days before Father McGlynn celebrated mass for the first time in five years, George wrote to Reverend Dawson, his friend of long standing, that he had "for some time believed Leo XIII to be a very great man; . . . Whether he will ever read my letter [*The Condition of Labor*] I cannot tell, but he has been acting as though he had not only read it, but had recognised its force."[20]

In the same letter George credited the Pope with quieting the toryism of Archbishop Corrigan and stopping the fight against the public school.

George and McGlynn had had very little to do with each other after 1888 when they had split over George's support of Cleveland and over McGlynn's belief that the United Labor Party should persevere. McGlynn and the Anti-Poverty Society had gone its own way after George had voluntarily withdrawn. McGlynn had continued to live the life of a priest, though excommunicated, and had continued to preach the single tax. The Anti-Poverty Society slowly lost its force, and George's opportunistic hopes in Cleveland were dashed. Not only was Cleveland defeated in 1888, but when he was re-elected in 1892 his mildly expressed free-trade policy was overshadowed by his use of Federal troops in the Pullman strike. By that time George's disappointment in the one Democratic president who had broken the hold on the White House which the Republicans were to maintain from the end of the Civil War to the Bull Moose days was complete.

In 1891, just as George began his final work, *The Science of Political Economy*, Pope Leo XIII issued his famous encyclical *On the Condition of Labor*. Though the Pope did not mention George by name, Archbishop Corrigan saw the letter as evidence in support of his own opposition to George and McGlynn. Henry George, Jr., writes that Cardinal Manning told him personally that the Pope's encyclical was indeed aimed at his father's teaching, "although he intimated that between the postulates and the deduction Henry George could drive a coach and four."[21] At any rate, George assumed that the encyclical was "aimed at us, and at us alone, almost,"[22] and proceeded to answer it with mixed feelings of honor at so being addressed. It gave him the opportunity to speak his piece once again on a national and international scale. In reply he set forth his principles in a long "Open Letter," completed in September, 1891, which was more .han double the length of the Pope's encyclical.

The Condition of Labor, an Open Letter to Pope Leo XIII is one of George's best written and soundly argued works and states very well the religious and ethical bases of his social philosophy. Published in October, 1891, in the United States, the United Kingdom, and Italy (in translation) at the same time,

George's book never received any answer from Rome, though a personal and handsome copy of the Italian translation had been presented to the Pope. Employing the editorial "we," as well as speaking for all who thought as he did, he said: "Our postulates are all stated or implied in your Encyclical. They are the primary perceptions of human reason, the fundamental teachings of the Christian faith" (3). The Pope's encyclical, for all it had in common with George's own views, did not stress equality and insist upon land reform which George felt were necessary if any real changes in labor's condition were ever to occur. In a letter to his son, George wrote that he had written "for such men as Cardinal Manning, General Booth and religious-minded men of all creeds."[23] *The Condition of Labor* repeated all the essential points of George's arguments developed in *Progress and Poverty* and the writings that preceded and followed his major work.

> To attach to things created by God the same right of private ownership that justly attaches to things produced by labor is to impair and deny the true rights of property. For a man who out of the proceeds of his labor is obliged to pay another man for the use of ocean or air or sunshine or soil, all of which are to men involved in the single term land, is in this deprived of his rightful property and thus robbed. (5)
>
> Clearly, purchase and sale cannot give, but can only transfer ownership. Property that in itself has no moral sanction does not obtain moral sanction by passing from seller to buyer.
>
> If right reason does not make the slave the property of the slave-hunter it does not make him the property of the slave-buyer. Yet your reasoning as to private property in land would as well justify property in slaves. To show this it is only needful to change in your argument the word land to the word slave. (25)

After much religious and historically oriented discussion in the first half of his argument, George turned in the third section of his "Open Letter" to current economic theories, indicating how he differed from trade unionism, communism, socialism, or anarchism. He then developed his argument in the fourth section by drawing together his social and religious points of view, saying that "the social question is at bottom a religious question" (67). (The phraseology is reminiscent of his address "The Crime of Poverty.")

After complimenting the Pope for lending his support to this point, he then says of the Pope's remedies that they "so far as they go are socialistic, and though the Encyclical is not without recognition of the individual character of man and of the priority of the individual and the family to the state, yet the whole tendency and spirit of its remedial suggestions lean unmistakably to socialism—extremely moderate socialism it is true; socialism hampered and emasculated by a supreme respect for private possessions; yet socialism still" (70-71). This point was ironic, since the Pope had already written that socialism fails "to see the order and symmetry of natural law" and "fails to recognize God" (61).

Continuing his argument, George then struck at the division of society into classes:

> For is it not clear that the division of men into the classes rich and poor has invariably its origin in force and fraud; invariably involves violation of the moral law; and is really a division into those who get the profits of robbery and those who are robbed; those who hold in exclusive possession what God made for all, and those who are deprived of his bounty? Did not Christ in all his utterances and parables show that the gross difference between rich and poor is opposed to God's law? Would he have condemned the rich so strongly as he did, if the class distinction between rich and poor did not involve injustice—was not opposed to God's intent? (83)

Listing the contradictions in the "moral teachings" of the Pope's encyclical (97-98), George concludes: "you give us equal rights in heaven, but deny us equal rights on earth! . . . your Encyclical gives the gospel to laborers and the earth to the landlords" (98). In the language of his "Moses" address, he appeals: "Servant of the Servants of God! I call you by the strongest and sweetest of your titles. In your hands more than in those of any living man lies the power to say the word and make the sign that shall end an unnatural divorce, and marry again to religion all that is pure and high in social aspiration" (104). Such public sentiments were in marked contrast to George's opinions of the same year expressed in a personal letter just before he was confronted with the Pope's encyclical: "How sad it is to see a church in all its branches offering men stones instead of bread, and thistles instead of figs. From Protestant preachers to Pope, avowed teachers of Christianity are with few exceptions preaching alms giving or socialism, and ignoring the simple remedy of justice."[24]

Despite his many Roman Catholic friends and associates, clerical and lay, at home and abroad, Henry George's relations with Rome were at best uneven and uncertain. It was touch and go for many years as to whether or not his works were to be included in the *Index librorum prohibitorum*.

III   *Henry George's Last Ten Years: The Single Tax*

By the end of 1887 Henry George's career as a leader of social reform took its final turn. His November 19th editorial in the *Standard*, "The Chicago Tragedy," which followed the disastrous defeat at the polls, and the October 8th editorial which may have helped to cause that defeat, explained George's position regarding the convicted anarchists. Explanations did no good, however; he was called a traitor by labor partisans and by the labor press. Many of his former supporters and associates in the United Kingdom, except some of the Fabians and religious social reformers, joined their American compatriots in condemning him for siding with the establishment's opinion of who were to be held responsible for the deaths that occurred during the Haymarket Riot. In the United States George's opposition came not only from the right and from the Catholic Church but also from many workingmen's organizations.

From 1887 onward, most of George's activity as a writer and thinker was devoted to his editorials in the *Standard*; to his lectures and addresses, including several tours abroad; to his reply to Pope Leo and his attack upon Herbert Spencer in *A Perplexed Philosopher*; and to his posthumously published *The Science of Political Economy*. His political activities centered around the single tax movement in the late 1880's and early 1890's, his support of free trade policies in Congress, and finally his return to active campaigning in the 1897 New York mayoralty race, the major cause of his sudden death.

The single tax movement began gradually to gather force through 1887, mainly as a result of the work of a New York lawyer named Thomas Shearman; and George's last editorial in the *Standard* for the same year showed how completely he had adopted the phrase and the idea as a rallying point for himself. The editorial was entitled "Socialism vs the Single Tax." Over a year later, after another trip abroad, George described frankly what he believed the single tax to mean: "The term single tax does not really express all that a perfect term would convey. It only suggests the fiscal side of our aims. . . . Before we adopted this name, people, even intelligent people, insisted on believing we meant to divide land up. . . . Since we have used the term single tax this sort of misinterpretation seems to have almost entirely disappeared. . . ."

George was not completely happy with the term because it failed to communicate his socio-economic and religio-ethical creed in its entirety, but it had its advantages—especially in the slogan-ridden world of popular political propaganda. He did not like the restrictions implied by the narrowness of the term. George thought, nevertheless, that the term associated the single tax movement with "those great Frenchmen, ahead of their time, who, over a century ago, proposed the *impôt unique* as the great means for solving social problems and doing away with poverty. . . . Our proper name, if it would not seem too high flown, 'would be freedom men,' or 'liberty men,' or 'natural order men,' for it is on establishing liberty, on removing restrictions, on giving natural order full play, and not on any mere fiscal change that we base our hopes of social reconstruction."

"This idea," he went on, "is more fully expressed in the term single tax than it would be in land rent tax or any other such phrase. We want as few taxes as possible, as little restraint as is conformable to that perfect law of liberty which will allow each individual to do what he pleases without infringement of the equal right of others."[25] The Henry George of *Progress and Poverty* was always present, even in the days of the single tax, which term he was one day to label a "misnomer" that somehow or other stuck. From 1888 to 1890, single tax clubs began to organize throughout the country. While George's relationship with labor organizations cooled, his standing with the middle class began to rise almost like one of his economic ratios.

Just after the 1888 election, George had the opportunity of returning to the United Kingdom for the fourth time. It was a quick trip and a hectic and busy stay. He was very well received and, as usual, very optimistic about the progress of his ideas throughout the British Isles. By Christmas he was back in New York. Three months later, however, he was abroad again for a longer stay, taking his wife and daughters with him and leaving his eldest son in charge of the *Standard*.

A letter from a leading Fabian, Sidney Webb, indicates better than anything else how George stood with the socialists in 1889:

> I am afraid that you will be denounced and attacked by the wilder kind of Socialist. . . . others beside myself are doing all we can to induce them to keep quiet, *as it would be fatal to arouse an antagonism between the Radical and Socialist parties.* Many of us have been working for years to keep the peace between them, & to bring them into line on practical politics. . . .
>
> Now I want to implore your forbearance. When you are denounced as a traitor, & what not, by Socialist newspapers; and "heckled" by Socialist questioners, or abused by Socialist orators, it will be difficult not to denounce Socialism in return. But do not do so. They will be only the noisy fringe of the Socialist Party who will do this, & it will be better for the cause which we both have at heart, if you can avoid accentuating your differences with Socialists.[26]

Though the break with the Socialists was fairly obvious, George's four-month visit, his longest since 1882, went well. His speaking schedule was heavy, but it was not so concentrated as it was during his short tour at the end of 1888. As usual, his most successful meetings were in Scotland where his blend of religio-ethical ideas and socio-economic reform plans went over well. His older addresses, like "Moses," were accompanied by "Thy Kingdom Come," his very stirring and effective sermon delivered in the Glasgow City Hall. He had begun his tour in London with "Thou Shalt Not Steal," his repeatedly successful speech on the Eighth Commandment, which, dating from 1884, he had delivered impressively in New York City to the second public meeting of the Anti-Poverty Society in May, 1887. The speech was always a success because it answered the question of who really were the land stealers, the landlords or the reformers. The Scottish Land Restoration League audiences, of course, already knew the answer. Aside from farewell meetings in London, George ended his tour with "The Land for the People," delivered in Ireland in the summer just before his return to the United

States; the title of the address was one which Davitt had used for a speech to an English audience in 1883.

George was well on his way in 1889 to becoming the elder statesman of Land Reform in Europe. An interview in the *Pall Mall Gazette* with Leo Tolstoy sounded this note more clearly than anything else: "In thirty years private property in land will be as much a thing of the past as now is serfdom. England, America and Russia will be the first to solve the problem. . . . Henry George had formulated the next article in the programme of the progressist Liberals of the world."[27]

When the Paris Conference for land reform met in June, that international body elected Henry George its honorary president. As an outgrowth of the conference, about which George had mixed feelings, the Universal Land Federation was organized: George was named world leader. Not himself an active organizer of the new international federation, he was nevertheless informed about its affairs and asked to help create a world-wide list of individuals, organizations, and publications interested in the cause of land and tax reform. After he went back to the British Isles, he returned to America with invitations to visit Australia and New Zealand. His role as an international elder statesman, his world-wide honors, even his influence on political and economic affairs, dwarfed his stature at home.

On his return to New York, he received a fine welcome, but what cheered him most was the news that single tax petitions to Congress were growing steadily. Several large individual subscriptions soon put the *Standard* in good financial condition, and the paper became the hub of the single tax movement. Between George's return from England in the summer and his departure for Australia early in 1890, the *Standard* proclaimed in brief in a box on its front page as a regular feature of the paper, a three-point program for reform:

> "The Standard" is an exponent of the principles and a weekly record of important facts affecting social problems and rational politics. It especially advocates the following great reforms:
>
> *THE SINGLE TAX. This means the abolition of all taxes on labor or the products of labor, that is to say, the abolition of all taxes save one tax levied on the value of land irrespective of improvements.*

FREE TRADE. Not "tariff reform," but real free trade; that is, as perfect freedom of trade with all the world as now exists between the states of our union.

BALLOT REFORM. No humbug envelope system; but the real Australia system, the first requisite of which is the exclusive use of elections of official ballots furnished by the state and prepared and cast by the voter in compulsory secrecy.

Hopes were high that Congress could be influenced. And though *Protection or Free Trade* was finally read into the Congressional Record in 1892, those hopes were to remain largely unfulfilled.

One of George's first articles on his return from England had been devoted to Edward Bellamy's *Looking Backward* and the new Nationalist Clubs that were becoming very popular and very numerous as a result of Bellamy's book, second only to *Uncle Tom's Cabin* in its influence upon American social ideas. Like Mrs. Stowe's book, but unlike *Progress and Poverty*, *Looking Backward* was indeed a novel and not a treatise on political economy. Unlike Mrs. Stowe's book, however, it belonged to a particular literary genre of great popularity in the last decade of the nineteenth century. Its utopianism, though similar in some ways to George's own dreams for the perfect and just society, was socialistic and literary or artistic rather than individualistic and economic or pragmatic. *Looking Backward*, George wrote, "is a castle in the air, with clouds for its foundation . . . a popular presentation of the dream of state socialism, and in its failure to indicate any way of 'getting there,' does not differ from the more serious socialistic works which have supplied its suggestion." "Nevertheless," he wrote, "it is doing, and will do, great good." "That it is giving a strong impulse to socialism—the idea of effecting social improvement by government paternalism—is probably true. But socialism is far better than the contented acquiescence in suffering and wrong without thought of improvement in general conditions."[28]

Granting *Looking Backward* its contribution to the general movement for social reform, George and many of his supporters could not accept Bellamy's abridgement of laissez-faire economics. By this time, George had cut himself off almost completely from any truly socialistic thought, but he was still the staunch defender of the downtrodden and would not thwart any movement that would lessen in any way the suffering of human beings. He was convinced that the social revolution then beginning could not help but accept his principles, his theory, and his remedy as the only means by which its final success could be assured. Clearly never a Marxist, by the last decade of the nineteenth century it would have been difficult for an impartial judge to conclude that George was even in the broadest sense a Christian Socialist. Long right of Morris, George was ideologically not even so far left as Tolstoy, much less the Bellamyites in America or the Fabians in England; but George found great satisfaction in their influence upon socio-economic ideas. Essentially, he had more in common with Emerson than with Charles Fourier, or any of Fourier's American disciples like Horace Greeley. Thomas Jefferson remained his master. George dreamed an American dream in an American tradition.

Before George's departure for Australia in February, 1890, he made a number of lecture tours through the eastern United States, speaking often to single tax clubs. While he had had already the support of William Lloyd Garrison, Jr., in New England, by 1889 the young Hamlin Garland also became active in support of George's program, serving as the president of a single-tax club in Boston. Moreover, Garland's admiration for George the man and for George's ideas was lasting.

Finishing his tour in December, George set his affairs in order and left with his wife and daughters for Australia, going overland to San Francisco via St. Louis, New Mexico, and Los Angeles. Everywhere George was warmly and often enthusiastically received. In San Francisco in early February, he spoke twice to packed houses and "wild applause." Addressing himself to "Justice the Object—Taxation the Means" in Metropolitan Hall, he said:

> We call ourselves to-day single tax men. It is only recently, within a few years, that we have adopted that title. It is not a new title; over a hundred years ago there arose in France a school of philosophers and patriots—Quesnay, Turgot, Condorcet, Dupont—the most illustrious men of their time, who advocated, as the cure for all social ills, the *impôt unique*, the single tax.
>
> We here, on this western continent, as the nineteenth century draws to a close, have revived the same name, and we find enormous advantages in it.

We used to be confronted constantly by the question: "Well, after you have divided the land up, how do you propose to keep it divided?" We don't meet that question now. The single tax has, at least, this great merit: it suggests our method; it shows the way we would travel—the simple way of abolishing all taxes, save one tax upon land values.[29]

The address was directed mainly at the fiscal and political sides of George's single tax and was illustrated with biographical reminiscences. Following his usual style, he concluded on a Biblical and religious note.

George's reception and impact in 1890 in the city in which he had written *Progress and Poverty* and in which he had first come into prominence was equaled by his reception and his impact in New Zealand and Australia, if not surpassed. Sir George Grey, who had written glowingly from New Zealand of *Progress and Poverty* when he had first read the Author's Edition which George had sent to him ten years before, was in person all that George had expected. Grey's letters to George and his reply after their brief but extremely warm visit attest to the lasting friendship, the understanding, and the mutual admiration they had for each other and which had been sealed by their meeting: "You have expanded a spark," Grey wrote, "into a blaze of thought and of unselfish conceptions which is spreading to every part, and ennobling countless minds."[30]

In general, the globe-encircling trip was going well. Australia was Mrs. George's birthplace and the destination of George's first voyage from home aboard the *Hindoo* as a young, unknown, and inexperienced cabin boy. Although hectic and poorly organized, the visit stirred their emotions deeply. Coming thirty-five years after George's early adventure, the Australian tour was the high point of the entire voyage. The fact that he was then a world-famous figure only increased the excitement by supplementing private associations with public acclaim.

Leaving Australia, George and his family made their way from India through the Red Sea to Italy, France, and finally England. The visit made clear once and for all, however, that George still stood well with Protestant and radical organizations but that labor and socialist groups and he had drifted far apart. Back in New York in September, he attended the first National Single Tax League of the United States. On September 2nd, just after his arrival, George was greeted by thirty-five hundred people and spoke on the question of free trade. The meeting was simultaneously a kind of celebration of George's fifty-first birthday and a welcome-home party.

The end of 1890 was a time for summing up the accomplishments of three decades of writing, speaking, and teaching. In that time, which began with his coming of age, he had grown from the writer of that brotherly millennial letter to his sister to the father of the single tax movement. Emerson's sphinx had been answered many times. Perhaps, he felt, the "promised Millennium" was at least a little nearer than it had been at the beginning of the Civil War.

When George had returned from his round-the-world trip in September, he had planned to do some writing, but lecture tours in New England and Texas took up much of his time. Then came a serious stroke. Though he made a remarkable recovery, the strain and pressure of his busy life were beginning to tell—even on his strong constitution. Well rested by February, when he returned from Bermuda where he had been taken to recuperate, he now had the opportunity to devote himself to the kind of thought that had preceded and accompanied the composition of *Progress and Poverty* in the late 1870's. The political activity that had taken almost all of his time since his entry into the 1886 mayoralty campaign had slipped into the background, and George was in 1890 no longer at the center of labor politics. He began to work on what was intended to be his magnum opus, *The Science of Political Economy*. He felt that the time had now come for a theoretical reclarification of his ideas because so many of his concepts had become clouded in the popular press during the heat of political campaigning.

While much of the remaining six years of George's life was taken up with *A Perplexed Philosopher* and *The Science of Political Economy*—both discussed in the next section of this chapter—his death was to occur in a more public, more spectacular, and more typical way than at the writing desk. In 1897, finally working away full time on his last book, George heard rumors about the possibility of his running for mayor of the soon-to-be-expanded city of Greater New York. Seriously stressing his physical condition and the need for time to complete his book, he did his best to avoid the invitation to be the independent candidate for mayor. After he finally had made up his mind to accept, however, none of the medical advice which said that the campaign would be fatal could persuade him not to so engage all his energies.

When he formally accepted the nominations of several political groups and organizations at a large meeting at Cooper Union, he rose to the occasion:

> I have not sought this nomination directly or indirectly. It has been repugnant to me. My line lay in a different path, and I hoped to tread it; but I hold with Thomas Jefferson that while a citizen who can afford to should not seek office, no man can ignore the will of those with whom he stands when they have asked him to come to the front and represent a principle.
>
> . . . .
>
> A little while ago it looked to me at least that the defeat that the trusts, the rings and money power, grasping the vote of the people, had inflicted on William Jennings Bryan (applause) was the defeat of everything for which the fathers had stood, of everything that makes this country so loved by us, so hopeful for the future. It looked to me as though Hamilton had triumphed at last, and that we were fast verging upon a virtual aristocracy and despotism. You ask me to raise the standard again (applause); to stand for that great cause; to stand as Jefferson stood in the civil revolution in 1800. I accept. (Applause. Three cheers for Henry George were called for and given with cries of "And you will be elected, too!")
>
> I believe I shall be elected. (Applause.) I believe, I have always believed, that last year many so-called Democrats fooled with the principles of the Chicago platform, but that there was a power, the power that Jefferson invoked in 1800, that would cast aside like chaff all that encumbered and held it down; that unto the common people, the honest democracy, the democracy that believes that all men are created equal, would come a power that would revivify, not merely this imperial city, not merely the State, not merely the country, but the world. (Vociferous applause.)[31]

The newly organized party in support of George called itself, at his suggestion, "The Party of Thomas Jefferson." Once again it was an intense campaign, with George's friends doing their best to keep his share of the work to a minimum. But rallying the dissident elements to one banner was not an easy task. Three other major candidates were in the field, including Seth Low, the reform Republican, of whom George said on the night before his death: "I am not with Low. He is a Republican and is fighting the machine, which is all very good as far as it goes. But he is an aristocratic reformer; I am a democratic reformer. He would help the people; I would help the people to help themselves."[32] Low finished second, ahead of his party's machine-picked candidate.

Five days before the election, after four speeches in widely separated parts of the city, George returned at midnight to party headquarters at the Union Square Hotel. Exhausted, he went to bed only to awake during the early morning hours with a supposed case of indigestion, but he suffered a stroke soon after. Paralyzed but conscious for several hours, he was dead by morning, his final campaign and his last book both unfinished. He had died as he had lived, speaking and writing. The politician and the philosopher had been active to the very end in both of his callings. The writer, the thinker, and the political campaigner had spoken as one in the first of the four speeches he delivered the evening before his death:

> What I stand for and what my labor has been, I think you know. I have labored many years to make the great truth known, and they are written down in the books. What I stand for is the principle of true Democracy, the truth that comes from the spirit of the plain people and was given to us and is embodied in the philosophy of Thomas Jefferson. The Democracy of Jefferson is simple and good, and sums up the majesty of human rights and boundaries of government by the people. . . .
>
> Slowly but surely the Democracy of Jefferson has been strayed from, has been forgotten by the men who were, by its name, given office and power among the people. Error and wrong have been called by the name of truth, and the harvest of wrong is upon this land. There are bosses and trusts and sumptuary laws. Labor-saving machinery has been turned like captured cannon, against the ranks of labor, until labor is pressed to earth under the burden!
>
> And must no one rise up in the land of liberty when labor must humbly seek, as a boon, the right to labor?[33]

In the days that have come after the Henry George-like New Deal, the current right to labor or right to work and anti-poverty laws, and President Johnson's "Great Society," we may wonder as much at the language he chose as we may at the ideas. The problems and many of the catch-words are still, after all, the same. "What I stood for," he said that last night with the tone of a Hebrew prophet and a Jeffersonian, "is the equal rights of all men!"

IV *The Last Writings of Henry George*

After his reply to Pope Leo and the death of the *Standard*, George's writing oscillated from his books to free-lance journalism and back to his books again. In 1892 he published *A Perplexed Philosopher*, his attack on Herbert Spencer. Returning to *The Science of Political Economy*, which he had set aside for the reply to Leo and for the refutation of Spencer, George developed a large part of that work only to abandon it with the coming of the 1896 presidential election which he covered as a special correspondent and political analyst for the New York *Journal*. His series of articles was climaxed by "Shall the Republic Live?" which was printed the day before the election. After Bryan, whom George had supported and had predicted would win, had in fact lost, he returned to *The Science of Political Economy* until wooed away in order to make his last campaign.

In some ways *A Perplexed Philosopher* is as much a companion to the letter to the Pope as *Protection or Free Trade* is to *Social Problems*. His reply to Pope Leo, which stated George's understanding of the relation of social reform to the Christian ethic, was an attack upon the Pope's reasoning and clericalism, an attack by freedom and liberalism upon restraint and conservatism—enlightened as it may have been. *A Perplexed Philosopher* stated George's understanding of the relation of social reform to materialism. It was an attack upon the "Pope of the Agnostics" and evolutionary thinking, an attack by freedom and liberalism upon license and reaction. The premises and logic of both "popes" were called into question.

In *A Perplexed Philosopher*, George was not interested in debating biological evolution, but he would not tolerate the transfer of Darwinian theories of biological development to social philosophy and social development. The "essential fatalism" of Spencer's philosophy led, in George's mind, to the toleration of any social ill—a reactionary position with which he had no patience.[34]

The quarrel with Spencer had begun long before the 1890's. Spencer was more than a symbol of the enemy: he was the enemy. George and his disciples often quoted Spencer in support of the single tax and of George's general ideas about land. He is quoted in support of the argument in *Progress and Poverty*. Spencer's *Social Statics*, though published in 1850, was reviewed with *Progress and Poverty* in England early in the 1880's because of obvious similarities. But Spencer denied his support in any way, even denying to George face-to-face that the Irish were in the right or at least had a good case. Spencer finally recanted publicly and prepared a new edition of *Social Statics* purged of any suggestion that he had supported radical ideas about land. To George, Spencer had been dishonest as a writer, as a philosopher, and as a man. He had been irresponsible and self-contradictory. And in essence, George had a sound complaint: Spencer's actions had been questionable. He had kept a book in print for forty years without making any attempt to indicate that he no longer entertained some of its major contentions or obvious implications. An uneven attack, *A Perplexed Philosopher* is not to be listed among George's best books, however justified.

Toynbee's very early rejection of George's ideas, Huxley's more recent onslaught in *Nineteenth Century* in 1890, and Spencer's public turnabout made Spencerianism and many late nineteenth-century points of view logical targets for George. He tried his best to define a late eighteenth-century idealism of a Jeffersonian kind while attacking the *Zeitgeist* of the late nineteenth. *A Perplexed Philosopher* is divided into three parts: "Declaration," "Repudiation," and "Recantation." The first two parts have six chapters each; the third, thirteen. A short introduction and a brief conclusion state the "reason for" and the "moral of" the examination. The book is often bad-tempered and sometimes tedious while occasionally brilliant. George was again in the middle. His laissez-faire individualism was informed by the Judeo-Christian ethic whereas essentially Spencer's was not. Spencer, George contended, was clearly materialistic, like the socialists; his laissez-faire social philosophy was that of the jungle, unjust and illogical—reason enough for the rapid rise of socialistic movements for reform that cared more for the progress of the community or social organization than for the survival of the fittest.

Against the "scientific" Spencer, George appeared almost a democratic socialist and certainly a Christian. "In his first book, written when he [Spencer] believed in God, in a divine order, in a moral sense, and which he has now emasculated, he does appear as an honest and fearless, though somewhat too careless a thinker. But that part of our examination which crosses what is now his distinctive philosophy shows him to be, as a philosopher ridiculous, as a man contemptible—a fawning Vicar of Bray, clothing in pompous phraseology and arrogant assumption logical confusions so absurd as to be comical" (274-75). The "Pope of the Agnostics" was "the foremost of those who in the name of science eliminate God and degrade man, taking from human life its highest dignity and deepest hope" (276).

Against the Pope of Rome, George appeared the Christian democrat, a radical and evangelical individualist against socialism and the pious status quo. The open letter to the Pope had been a restatement of his views from one perspective and in opposition to a particular kind of denouncement. *A Perplexed Philosopher* restated clearly George's opinion that private property in land should be abolished, and it also implied strongly that personal income taxes were unfair and unnecessary. It was as much a rejection of materialism as his open letter had been a rejection of clericalism, though it was not so well-presented nor so well-written and even-tempered as the earlier reply of the previous year. George was inclined to be less patient with a man who had apparently retreated from an enlightened social view and who was a materialist than he was with a man who had apparently made an advance of some sort toward an enlightened social view and who was the spiritual leader of millions of Christians. His attitude toward his respective opponents affected the style and the worth of his two books accordingly.

All students of George agree that *A Perplexed Philosopher* does contain one particularly effective, well-written, and well-argued chapter—one capable of standing independent of the book. The chapter is "Compensation," the eleventh in Part III. It is a firm and brilliant restatement of the reasons for the confiscation of private property in land without payment or compensation to the supposed owners. George's supporters in the United States and abroad asked at the time for separate publication of the chapter in pamphlet form because they thought it so well done as to be helpful in the daily struggle to propagate the ideas of George's total view.

George half regretted writing both *A Perplexed Philosopher* and *The Condition of Labor*. The two polemical replies had cost him time that he thought might have been better spent on *The Science of Political Economy*. Many of his critics, friendly and otherwise, have thought that the posthumous publication of an unfinished work from a dying body and a tired spirit was an unfortunate error. *The Science of Political Economy* should not really be compared without care to *Progress and Poverty*, a literary shot heard round the world. In all fairness it is not a bad book, but only an unfinished and unsettled one that was never destined to receive the undivided attention of its author. Whatever the reason may be for George's unwillingness or inability to work upon his last book as intensely as he had on his masterwork, the fact still remains that the final result in each case was as different in kind as the method of composition.

George worked intermittently on the book from 1891 until his death, and its divisions and organization in no way reflect the order in which its various parts were written. *The Science of Political Economy* begins with a general introduction and is followed by five "Grand Divisions" or Books, each with an introduction of its own and various well-indexed chapters: I. "The Meaning of Political Economy"; II. "The Nature of Wealth"; III. "The Production of Wealth"; IV. "The Distribution of Wealth"; and V. "Money—The Medium of Exchange and Measure of Value." According to his eldest son:

The last three books were largely written in the summer of 1897, but were not completed at the time of Mr. George's death; and when the work was published as it had been left by his hand, many critics spoke of the evidences of declining powers in the last three divisions and especially in the broken and even rough places in the part on money. The truth is that "The Science of Political Economy" as posthumously published is the best example that can be found of Henry George's method of work; for the last three divisions or "books" present much of his earlier drafting of the general work. The money division was written in 1894 and 1895, as dates on the rough-draft manuscript and in note-books indicate. The really last work he did was in smoothing and polishing the first two divisions, which Dr. Taylor assured him were equal in force, clearness and finish to his earlier high-water performance of "Progress and Poverty"; and in his opinion his own judgement concurred.[35]

Contemporary reviewers, as well as subsequent students of George's work, did not feel that *The Science of Political Economy* was really a good final statement of his philosophy; but it would have been impossible for George to have surpassed *Progress and Poverty*, especially since he had not altered any of the essential points of view expressed in his younger and more fiery major work. A. T. Hadley in the *Yale Review* more succinctly than anyone else sums up the reactions of those who were unfriendly to George's ideas:

> Henry George was a great preacher. *Progress and Poverty* is one of the most eloquent volumes of sermons which has appeared in the English language. But in proportion as George passes from the field of oratory into the field of science, his work becomes less good. He criticises his predecessors with no sparing hand, but he lays himself open to the same kind of criticism in far greater measure than they do. With all its claims of novelty, the book has little which is really new, unless it be a somewhat commonplace metaphysics within which the author tries to frame his economic system. Subtract this, and we have simply a new edition of *Progress and Poverty*, less well written, *plus* a number of rather disconnected utterances on money and kindred topics, logical enough when the author sticks close to Smith and Mill, and less so in proportion as he departs from those models. For this reason it is quite impossible to review the book *in extenso*. This is not the first time a good preacher has proved himself a poor conversationalist. Those of us who have admired George for his brilliant earlier work and for his unblemished personal character can only regret that this last book was ever written and desire that it may be forgotten as soon as possible.[36]

The Science of Political Economy is not a whole book, even less so than *A Perplexed Philosopher*. The faults of George's last work, however, are not those of his book on Spencer. The book is partly autobiographical, partly critical, partly historical, and partly a review of *Progress and Poverty* and its reception by those for and against him. There is little in it that is truly new so far as George's religio-economic thinking is concerned. It is not the definitive statement of his views that he wished to write, and it suffers from the many interruptions that caused it to be set aside for other matters and events of equal interest to its author during its composition. Nevertheless, it is well argued and well written, deserving the praise that Georgists have given it.

In *The Science of Political Economy*, George exploits the leviathan metaphor of Hobbes and Melville by writing that "the body politic, or Leviathan" of which every citizen is a part, is dependent upon "the body economic, or Greater Leviathan." "This body economic, or Greater Leviathan, always precedes and always underlies the body politic or Leviathan. . . . And from this relation of dependence upon the body economic, the body politic can never become exempt" (27). It was this "Greater Leviathan" that "Saint George" had tried to make fast, if not overpower, with his social and economic theories.

As in all his works, George very effectively in *The Science of Political Economy* stresses man's ability to master his economic difficulties through the power of reason. He refers to man as "the only progressive animal" and emphasizes man's "power of 'thinking things out,' of 'seeing the way through'—the power of tracing causal relations." Typically, he presses his point through a habitual stylistic device—the homely and humorous analogy: "The dog and cow sometimes look wise enough to be meditating on anything. If they really could bother their heads with such matters or express their ideas in speech, they would probably say that such sequences are invariable, and then rest. But man is impelled by his endowment of reason to seek behind fact or cause. For that something cannot come from nothing, that every consequence implies a cause, lies at the very foundation of our perception of causation. To deny or ignore this would be to cease to reason—which we can no more cease in some sort of fashion to do than we can cease to breathe" (56). Here again is seen George's dedication to Jeffersonian and Emersonian modes of thought and expression, the theme of "The Sphinx" poem which he had quoted more than thirty years before, and the compulsion to go "behind fact or cause" which is reminiscent of Melville's deep dive for the "little lower layer." His philosophical linking of the barter in ideas through speech or language with that of goods through money is a fine insight that is finally developed late in the book. To see the spiritual force behind natural or material objects is to see the economic forces behind politics. As Adam discovered in the beginning, the naming of things properly is important. There is an embryonic esthetic theory in George's elucidation of that well-known American maxim, "money talks." George's definition of money is just that:

> Whatever in any time and place is used as the common medium of exchange is money in that time and place.
>
> There is no universal money. While the use of money is almost as universal as the use of languages, and it everywhere follows general laws as does the use of languages, yet as we find language differing in time and place, so do we find money differing. In fact, as we shall see, money is in one of its functions a kind of language—the language of value. (494)

In writing about the genesis of *Progress and Poverty*, George recalled that "While in the East [in 1869-70], the contrast of luxury and want that I saw in New York appalled me, and I left for the West feeling that there must be a cause for this, and that if possible I would find out what it was. Turning over the matter in my mind amid pretty constant occupation, I at length found the cause in the treatment of land as property" (201). From 1871 with *Our Land and Land Policy* to 1879 and *Progress and Poverty*, George developed a theory and found a remedy which he still was convinced were right in 1897.

In *The Science of Political Economy*, George repeated and also enlarged upon his theories, offering additional analogies to explain value. He said that to the political economist, land in reality is "not wealth at all" (265). He compared the value attached to land to the value attached to works of art:

> The value that attaches to land with the growth of civilization is an example of the same principle which governs in the case of a picture by a Raphael or Rubens, or an Elgin marble. Land, which in the economic sense includes all the natural opportunities of life, has no cost of production. It was here before man came, and will be here, so far as we can see, after he has gone. It is not produced. It was created.
>
> And it was created and still exists in such abundance as even now far to exceed the disposition and power of mankind to use

it. Land as land, or land generally—the natural element necessary to human life and production—has no more value than air
as air. But land in special, that is, land of a particular kind or in
a particular locality, may have a value such as that which may
attach to a particular wine-glass or a particular picture or statue;
a value which unchecked by the possibility of production has no
limit except the strength of the desire to possess it. (255)

One can imagine what George's response would have been to
the moral of Tolstoy's parable, his famous short story "How
Much Land does a Man Need?" had he read it.

Like all of his works, *The Science of Political Economy* shows
George's eloquent and deep understanding of the nature of humanity and the progress of civilization—what might be called
social history—and his keen insights into the relation of economics to politics. He and his supporters were fond of quoting
Macauley's ironic observation that had powerful financial interests decided to block general acceptance of the law of gravita-
tion its truth would still be open to question.

The question that was being posed, however, was the one
which George addressed to the readers of the New York *Journal*
in November of 1896, "Shall the Republic Live?":

The banks are not really concerned about their legitimate business under any currency. They are struggling for the power of
profiting by the issuance of paper money, a function properly
and constitutionally belonging to the nation. The railroads are
not really concerned about the fifty-cent dollar, either for themselves or their employes. They are concerned about their power
of running the Government and making and administering the
laws. The trusts and pools and rings are not really concerned
about any reduction in the wages of their workmen, but for their
own power of robbing the people. The larger business interests
have frightened each other, as children do when one says,
"Ghost!" Let them frighten no thinking man.[37]

But the economic ghosts of yesterday were no less powerful
then than they are today. Bryan lost the election, labor was cruci-
fied after a fashion on a cross of gold, and George's question
remained unanswered. One would not be far wrong in saying
that the ghosts still haunt the politico-economic nightmare that is
often America's public opinion life:

Would they [the voters] not expect to have every man who stood prominently for freedom denounced as an Anarchist, a communist, a repudiator, a dishonest person, who wished to cut down just debts? Is not this so now? Would they not expect to hear predictions of the most dire calamity overwhelming the country if the power to rob the masses was lessened ever so little? Has it not been so in every struggle for greater freedom that they can remember or have ever read of?[38]

George's climactic article in his series for the *Journal* demonstrates more clearly than anything he wrote in his later years that he was the same man he had always been, that he had not ceased to fight them with any less zeal than before.

Though George wrote a little peevishly as a disappointed preacher-prophet in *A Perplexed Philosopher* and in *The Science of Political Economy*, he did so characterize his own background as to place himself undeniably in the tradition of the American writer whose Yale College and his Harvard was either before the mast of a sailing vessel or under the masthead of a newspaper. George's voice came straight from the forecastle and swept aft over the whole length and breadth of the ship of state. His role was that of the prophet Elijah and not of the priest-kings or Ahabs of this world:

What were their training and laborious study worth if it could be thus ignored, and if one who had never seen the inside of a college, except when he had attempted to teach professors the fundamentals of their science, whose education was of the mere common-school branches, whose *alma mater* had been the forecastle and the printing-office, should be admitted to prove the inconsistency of what they had been teaching as a science? It was not to be thought of. And so while a few of these professional economists, driven to say something about "Progress and Poverty," resorted to misrepresentation, the majority preferred to rely upon their official positions in which they were secure by the interests of the dominant class, and to treat as beneath contempt a book circulating by thousands in the three great English-speaking countries and translated into all the important modern languages. Thus the professors of political economy seemingly rejected the simple teachings of "Progress and Poverty," refrained from meeting with disproof or argument what it had laid down, and treated it with contemptuous silence. (204)

Unfrightened and unmoved by economic ghosts or by silent academic spirits, George had had his say and many had listened.

CHAPTER 6

The Impact and the Influence
of Henry George: A Final Appraisal

I Mourning, Appreciation, and Contemporary Assessment

HENRY GEORGE'S DEATH shocked everyone, except possibly George who had expected it would come soon and so prepared himself. He had made his will the previous May in the presence of his two sons, leaving everything he had—little that it was—to his wife. The reactions of the world to his death indicate very well the impact and influence he had upon the world he so dramatically left behind.

George's body lay in state in Grand Central Palace all day Sunday, October 31st. According to various contemporary estimates, from twenty-five to one hundred thousand people passed the bier: fifty thousand is the figure most often mentioned in the papers in the days and weeks that followed. The *Irish World* estimated that at the peak of this tribute about six thousand people passed each hour. The lowest estimate of those who saw the casket was one hundred and twenty-five thousand, the highest in the hundreds of thousands. The *Irish World* of November 6, 1897, said that "The popular demonstration at his funeral parade was imposing as it was unparalleled in this city, and his name has become a household word in two hemispheres." The *Times* said, "Call it what you will, hero-worship, but its object was truly a hero." The *Herald* said it was "unique." One paper compared the funeral to Lincoln's, another to Grant's. In the *Times*, Hamlin Garland was quoted as that "Not even Lincoln had a more glorious death than this humble man who died fighting for the real interests of his countrymen." The *Financial Post* of the same day (October 30, 1897) said "From a Stock Exchange point of view, his death removes a disturbing element in American political and industrial life," but even this comment was buried in the publication's recognition of George's accomplishments and personal integrity.

The general reaction of praise and mourning was overpowering. "Never for statesman or soldier," said still another newspaper, "was there so remarkable a demonstration of popular feeling. At least one hundred thousand persons passed before his bier and another hundred thousand were prevented from doing so only by the impossibility of getting near it. Unconsciously they indicated over his dead body the truth of the great idea to which his life was devoted, the brotherhood of man."

In the afternoon the hall was jammed to capacity. Congregationalist, Episcopalian, Catholic, and Jewish groups and clerics were present, including Father McGlynn. It was a solemn, largely spontaneous, and public demonstration of grief and respect as well as an organized tribute to a man who was loved and admired even more than he was listened to or understood. When Father McGlynn reaffirmed his belief in the ideas of Henry George, the awesome but silent excitement of the hour was broken. The cheers of thousands echoed through the hall, releasing pent-up emotions that had reached the breaking point by that late hour. Seemingly out of place, the cheers were the kind of acclaim that George, who never stood on ceremony, would have approved.

Through the late evening and into the night, the long funeral procession passed slowly downtown, leaving Grand Central Palace and moving down Madison and Third avenues to City Hall and over Brooklyn Bridge to Borough Hall where the casket was given over to the family for the private burial service of November 1st in Greenwood Cemetery in Brooklyn. The garland-covered and open hearse was drawn by sixteen black draped horses while a volunteer band played Chopin's "Funeral March" and "The Marseillaise." A long, winding line of people—the known and the unknown—from all walks of life followed the casket.[1] It was a ceremony of the sort rarely seen at any time. As still another paper put it, "The world yesterday paid the highest tribute, perhaps, it has ever paid to the quality of sincerity." In fact, if one note dominated the countless articles and obituaries following George's death, it was the universal acknowledgment of his honesty and goodness. The New York *Herald's*

Paris edition of October 31st said wryly in a cabled dispatch from New York, "All the obituaries in the newspapers are most flattering. It reminds one of the famous lines:—

> Seven cities claimed Homer dead
> Through which, living, Homer begged his bread."

Cities and towns all over the world, in almost every country, and on every continent, paid their respects. On his death and funeral alone, articles numbered well into the hundreds, perhaps well into the thousands. Even separate funeral services were held in London. The personal messages to the family of regret and condolence from friends, rivals, and contemporary people of note came in a steady stream.[2]

George's influence at home and abroad in the 1880's and 1890's was far-reaching and, perhaps, everlasting. Reminiscing in the early 1920's, Samuel Gompers, the outstanding leader of the American Federation of Labor, wrote in his autobiography, "Political action had no appeal for me, but I appreciated the movement [of 1886] as a demonstration of protest. The campaign was notable in that it united people of unusual abilities from many walks of life." This kind of reaction always was and always has been a characteristic of Henry George's appeal. "It proved," Gompers continued, "a sort of vestibule school for many who later undertook practical work for human betterment." There are Bernard Shaw's words, among those of many others, for the similar influence George had on the people of the British Isles. "Many leaders in the constructive work of the following years," Gompers went on, "were recruits of the Henry George Campaign." In 1886 Gompers had said, and he quoted himself in spite of his distaste for direct political action, "Now I come out for George as a trade unionist and intend to support him with all my might."[3]

A week after his death, George's old socialist friend and opponent, Henry Hyndman—after citing all the ways in which he disagreed with George and after summing up the major events in George's career—concluded his obituary article by saying, "He has died in a chivalrous attempt to accomplish the impossible without even organizing his forces for the struggle. In a period when the highest ideals of the United States seem to be swindling at home and braggadocio abroad, Henry George, with all his mistakes, gave us an example of an honest, modest, self-taught American whose success in catching the ear of the world never turned his head for a moment."[4]

Considering the fact that George was neither a convinced trade unionist nor a socialist, these are remarkable pronouncements. They were unsolicited. Hyndman's was, of course, a personal appreciation of the hour, but it was in a way a part of that response evidenced by one newspaper's coupling of George with Garibaldi, George Fox, Rousseau, Swedenborg, and Peter the Hermit as "prophets in fire and fools in wisdom." Such praise of George said little for his practical program or even for his educative influence, other than as a model of personal integrity. James Bartley represented a more balanced view, a view that was shared by others, and that anticipated Shaw's assessment. "It was 'Progress and Poverty,'" he wrote, "that gave birth to the Fabian Society."[5] Shaw in his letter to Hamlin Garland is also thankful that, unlike the doctrinaire socialist, he did not lose his perspective on Henry George—a perspective he shared with Sidney Webb—when his Georgist views developed into Marxist ones.

The final words about George's influence in his own time were best and most accurately written by J. A. Hobson in a fine, objective article finished shortly before George's death and published in the same year in which he died:

> The influence of George is not, however, to be measured by the number or zeal of the advocates of a wholesome policy of nationalisation of the land. It is rather to be traced in the energy which, during the last fifteen years, has freely flowed into many channels of land reform. . . .
>
> No doubt it is easy to impute excessive influence to the mouthpiece of a rising popular sentiment. George, like other prophets, cooperated with the "spirit of the age." But after this just allowance has been made, Henry George may be considered to have exercised a more directly powerful influence over English radicalism of the last fifteen years than any other man.[6]

George's impact on Tolstoy, his senior by many years, was profound and well-known, even in the 1890's:

> I have been acquainted with Henry George since the appearance of his "Social Problems." I read them, and was struck by the correctness of his main idea, and by the unique clearness and

power of his argument, which is unlike anything in scientific literature, and especially by the Christian Spirit, which also stands alone in the literature of science, which pervades the book. After reading it I turned to his previous work "Progress and Poverty," and with a heightened appreciation of its author's activity.[7]

In a letter written before George's death, Tolstoy said that, "If the Czar were to ask me what I should advise him to do, I would say to him: Use your autocratic power to abolish the landed property in Russia, and to introduce the single-tax system, and then give up your power and give the people a liberal constitution."[8] Shortly after George's death, Tolstoy outlined in six steps the "advantage" of George's system:

1. That no one will be deprived of the possibility of using land.
2. That idle men, possessing land, and forcing others to work for them, in return for the use of the land, will cease to exist.
3. That the land will be in the hands of those who work it and not of those who do not.
4. That the people, being able to work on the land, will cease to enslave themselves as laborers in factories and manufactories, and as servants in towns, and will disperse themselves about the country.
5. That there will be no longer any overseers and tax collectors in factories, stores, and custom-houses, but only collectors of payment for the land, which it is impossible to steal, and from which taxes may be most easily collected.
6 (and chiefly). That those who do not labor will be freed from the sin of profiting by the labors of others (in doing which they are often not to blame, being from childhood educated in idleness, and not knowing how to work); and from the still greater sin of every kind of falsehood and excuse to shift the blame from themselves; and that those who do labor will be delivered from the temptation and sin of envy, condemnation of others, and exasperation against those who do not work; and thus will disappear one of the causes of dissension between man and man.[9]

The affinity between George and Tolstoy can be traced quickly to their religiously oriented view of man. Tolstoy's commitment to the very same things which were most important to George also indicates why he was more fully in harmony with George than Shaw or others of an essentially non-religious turn of mind. The same thing in Tolstoy that drew him to Thoreau or Emerson (as different as these two Americans may be from George as individual people, thinkers, or writers) drew him to George: the spiritual evolution of man according to "higher laws." In fact, Tolstoy's American consciousness[10]—if his affinity for Emerson, Thoreau, William Lloyd Garrison, Edward Bellamy, and George can be so described—should cause one to pause over De Tocqueville's thesis about Russia and the United States in the years that were to come. George's last-ditch capitalism, as Marx called his economic theory, has enough in common with the social philosophies of Tolstoy, Thoreau, and Ruskin to make George—who also read and quoted De Tocqueville—a particularly interesting phenomenon and an important influence upon the growth of social reform in the intellectual and economic life of Russia and the United States, not to mention his incalculable impact on the British Isles and his ever-widening influence in Europe and Oceania. Professor Max Müller, his friend and host of the 1880's in England, even applied his doctrines to India and its land problems, and Müller was in his day a leading scholar in the western world on the subject of the Asian sub-continent.

Henry George's impact on social reform did not cease with his death or even shortly after, nor did recognition of his importance wane. The intensity of his own person was no more, but he had touched people who lived into the decades that began the twentieth century. Georgist or not, they carried with them something of the program and something of the energy of Henry George's remedy for social reform—writers and economists alike.

II   *The Single Tax, the Fels Fund, and Subsequent Developments*

During the 1890's much single tax agitation and organizational activity occurred, especially in certain states, such as Delaware, North Carolina, Colorado, and Massachusetts; it persisted until the beginning of World War I. Single-taxers were active in Washington, Texas, Oregon, and several other western states, including some Canadian provinces, and in Pennsylvania and New York.[11]

Perhaps the most interesting development at this time was the founding of the Joseph Fels Fund of America. It marked the last large-scale adventures of the single tax in politics and also encouraged the growth of the educative side of Henry

George's latter-day influence—the major developmental pattern which Georgist activity has followed since the second decade of the twentieth century.

Joseph Fels, the soap manufacturer, promised to contribute $25,000 a year for a period of five years to promote the single tax in the United States. He also pledged the same sum to support British single tax endeavors, adding pledges of various sums to aid the single-tax movement in other countries. Fels agreed to match every dollar raised by the movement itself up to the stipulated amount. He more than fulfilled his promise by exceeding the contribution of the movement by over $50,000. Activity was most intense in Oregon in the years just before the war. The Fund helped to organize meetings and conventions, supported the *Single Tax Review*, and aided the continued publication of George's works. Many state campaigns were launched in the hope that a single demonstration of the practicality of the single tax would be more effective than any number of debates over its theoretical worth. Most of the agitation was largely unsuccessful, for direct political victory was not forthcoming although political influence was not without some effect upon subsequent legislation and economic planning.[12]

Ten years after Fels' death, the Robert Schalkenbach Foundation continued the struggle in non-political action by carrying on the educational aspects of George's work. Through inexpensive re-publication of his writings, the Foundation hoped to continue the spread of his ideas. In 1932 the Henry George School of Social Science was founded by Oscar Geiger.[13] As time has gone on, the Schalkenbach Foundation and the Henry George School have joined forces.[14] George's works are always in print, and the school continues to teach in terms of them. There is a kind of justice in the existence of the Henry George School, for George always wanted to be a professor. It was the one title he once said (about the time of his address at the University of California in 1877) that he would rather have than any other. Instead, he earned the older and more honored title of prophet. Thus generally dismissed by the academies, he used the world for his classroom—finally getting a school of his own, interestingly enough, in the midst of the worst of the recurrent depressions he sought to remedy.

At the twenty-fifth anniversary dinner for *Progress and Poverty* in 1905, Hamlin Garland, the toastmaster, introduced in turn a series of speakers who testified to the already well-established impact of George's work and ideas. They included Edwin Markham, who read poems; Ernest Thompson Seton, who read three fables; Henry George, Jr., who discussed the history of *Progress and Poverty*; Dr. Richard Burton, who discussed the influence of the book on literature; William Lloyd Garrison, Jr., who discussed its plea for justice; Tom Johnson, a follower of George, long in Congress, who discussed its influence toward higher politics; Dr. Albert Shaw, who discussed its influence for humanity; Louis Post, who discussed its economic message; and William Jennings Bryan, who spoke on equal opportunity and referred to Tolstoy. *Progress and Poverty* had already become a classic, but not a dead one. One of Markham's poems deserves quotation because it amplifies the meaning of Bernard Shaw's letter which Garland read to the assembled guests:

The Hand of Privilege

It picks the pockets of the poor,
To make the Idle Few secure.
Three evil fingers, knotty and bent,
Are Profit, Interest, and Rent:
One, like a thorn upon the hand,
Is Private Ownership of Land:
And last the crooked and crafty thumb
Is pointing the poor to the world to come![15]

Though the man with the hoe had found his public defender, the poem is somewhat left of George, having something in common with an old anonymous poem that philosophical anarchists like to quote:

Surplus Value

The Merchant calls it Profit and winks the other eye;
The Banker calls it Interest and heaves a cheerful sigh;
The Landlord calls it Rent as he tucks it in his bag;
But the honest old Burglar—he simply calls it Swag.

Further left or not, both poems have a Georgist spirit and remind the reader of George's own comic irony in speeches given around the world.

III *Conclusion: Liberty, A World-View*

Barker concludes his biography of Henry George with what he calls "The Triple Legacy of Georgism," which is, in brief, "three types of belief in his ideas": (1) "the fiscal-reform Georgism of the single tax"; (2) "the political Georgism which entered into many varieties of reform activity"; and (3) "the moral and intellectual Georgism, of which Tolstoy and Hamlin Garland were eloquent early figures."[16] Barker goes on to say that the "quiet influence of Henry George" from 1920 to the present day "is to be discovered on two levels":

> On the visible surface of affairs is the persevering work of the fiscal Georgists, who win occasional reforms in city tax policy. Very close to that effort, yet different, is the continuing task of the propagation of ideas, in the line which Henry George and Francis Shaw began in 1882. The work done in America centers in New York, where the Schalkenbach Foundation supplies subsidies, and where George's books and speeches are distributed and journals issued year after year. . . .
>
> The deeper level of Henry George's influence on the modern world is the one . . . often forgotten to be his. The participation of free governments in the processes of social justice is now accepted everywhere as policy to be maintained. A desire for world-wide free trade recurs in our day; and many believe that a greater equality among the peoples of the earth, of access to its resources, would increase mankind's hope for mankind.[17]

Barker also quotes Franklin K. Lane, President Wilson's conservationist Secretary of the Interior: "Emerson, Henry George, and William James were a 'singular trio' in history, who in the future would be 'regarded not as literary men but as American social, spiritual, and economic philosophers'; and he [Lane] thought also that William James, Theodore Roosevelt, and Henry George were 'the three greatest forces of the last thirty years.'"[18]

Henry George's philosophy is essentially an American worldview, true to the tradition of the American Dream. He saw no reason why the entire world could not become—if men were willing—the promised land of milk and honey, like the fruitful and ever bountiful plains of North America. In fact, it was America's task to show how such promise could be fulfilled, since America had the greatest opportunity that any nation ever had had; it was America's task to lead the rest of the world, like a colossal Joshua, into the millennial actuality of that dream. George had hinted that he was Moses. Consequently, he continued to be simultaneously left and right of center; but very few people, whether followers of George or not, have the capacity to be politically left and spiritually right. It is the kind of non-conformity for which, as Emerson would say, the world whips men with its displeasure.

There is little for anyone to argue with in the essentials of the appreciations of George, whether by Tolstoy, Shaw, Lane, Dewey, Barker or several others who have recognized his important contribution to the advance of social reform. His message was his own, and many learned enough from it to enable them to go their own ways without the crippling effect discipleship often bestows. Very few, however, have been capable of the religio-economic unity that is George's.

George's style reflects his message. It is biblical in its cadence, thus matching the frequent quotations from the Bible and the way in which his major work, *Progress and Poverty*, has been received and perpetuated. His style is aphoristic, yet ample— natural but eloquent. A prophet cannot fail to be quotable. The simple diction and the simple message must go together; furthermore, they must be capable of expressing complicated and abstract theory in concrete terms. George's rounded style matches his rounded philosophy. The religio-economic nature of his ideas is expressed in the simple and proverbial presentation of involved and logical argument. Clarity is what counts. George's advice to his son is not only the kind of advice which a well-trained newspaperman would give and which most would-be writers would do well to heed, but it also describes his own method: "The fault of most young writers is that they are too stilted. Always prefer the short ordinary words and the simplest phrase. And without being ungrammatical or slangy, try to write about as you would talk—so as to be easy and natural."[19] It is good Shavian advice, and it is modern and American: the kind of method necessary for those who—as Hyndman had said—would catch the ear of the world.

Liberty was George's major theme. The spirit and the substance of his Fourth of July addresses in the decade that marked the centenary of the Declaration of Independence were echoed in the conclusion of *Progress and Poverty* that came at the end of that decade. Liberty was what America stood for—the whole world knew that. And Liberty was what he stood for—right to the end with the party of the democracy of Thomas Jefferson. It was only fitting that Emma Lazarus some two years *before* she wrote "The New Colossus," her celebrated poem, in order to aid the pedestal fund drive to prepare Bedloe's Island for France's gift of the Statue of Liberty should have written another sonnet on reading *Progress and Poverty*:

PROGRESS AND POVERTY
[After Reading Mr. Henry George's Book]

Oh splendid age when Science lights her lamp
At the brief lightning's momentary flame,
Fixing it steadfast as a star, man's name
Upon the very brow of heaven to stamp!
Launched on a ship whose iron-cuirassed sides
Mock storm and wave. Humanity sails free;
Gayly upon a vast, untrodden sea,
O'er pathless wastes, to ports undreamed she rides,
Richer than Cleopatra's barge of gold,
This vessel, manned by demi-gods, with freight
Of priceless marvels. But where yawns the hold
In that deep, reeking hell, what slaves be they,
Who feed the ravenous monster, pant and sweat,
Nor know if overhead reign night or day?[20]

This sonnet—on unfound freedom and liberty—did not win the poet the fame the later poem did, but the two poems are not unlike. George, it must be remembered, was not interested in commemorating liberty but in establishing it. The pedestal fund drive coincided with the publication of *Social Problems*, just as the Battle of the Little Big Horn in 1876 coincided ironically with the one-hundredth anniversary year of the famous declaration that brought about the War of Independence. George did not miss the irony of the first, whether or not he may have been aware of the second. Liberty was taking a high price. The ultimate task that George had set himself was to see that we got the genuine article.

In a very important way, Franklin K. Lane was wrong. His error is to be found in the limitation he placed upon "literary" when he said (intending to laud) that Emerson, George, and

William James would not be regarded in the future as literary men. His observation implied that the literary qualities or the art of their work was of slight consequence in comparison with what they had philosophized about. But as Emerson himself says, a man is half himself; the other half is his expression. And if the two halves could be separated, if the way in which Emerson, George, and James express themselves could be separated in actuality from what they say, then one should have to conclude that the success of each—even his lasting fame—is traceable to the way in which each puts his arguments, not in the arguments themselves. Of nobody more than George is this true. Any successful polemist must write well; and George, whose success in his own time was as great as any man's could ever be, was essentially a writer, an artist of the word, as good a proof as any that the old maxim the pen is mightier than the sword is true. With his pen he had re-created the war of independence—the socio-political revolution of modern times. It was George's art that most made him what he was. Of George's work, Emerson is once again the best judge: "Conscious utterance of thought by speech or action to any end is art." George's word certainly went marching on, and his word is his truth. He had consciously uttered it by speech and by act to the very end of his life. Its meaning and its influence are still alive.

Notes and References

Chapter One

1. Letter to Hamlin Garland, December 29, 1904, Henry George Collection (typed copy). Quoted in Archibald Henderson, *George Bernard Shaw, His Life and Works* (London, 1911), pp. 152-53. See also, Henderson, *George Bernard Shaw: Man of the Century* (New York, [1956]), pp. 215-17. Charles Albro Barker in *Henry George* (New York, 1955), p. 376, quotes Shaw's letter at greater length than I have. It was read aloud by Hamlin Garland at the twenty-fifth Anniversary Dinner for *Progress and Poverty*, January 24, 1905. See below, Chapter IV, 14n and the final paragraph, Chapter VI, Section II.

2. I take Thoreau to have intended a pun in his usual manner, which I have then parodied. For Thoreau and George "concord" and "brotherly love" are states of mind as well as cities. In his political campaigns and his speaking tours George often resorted to the pun in order to provoke his audiences. George's pun on "duke" and "duck," for instance, is one of the humorous features of his speeches in Scotland in the 1880's.

3. The phrase originates with Henry Hyndman, the British socialist who knew George in England and who was a Marxist. Quoted in Barker, p. 357.

4. Sea Journal 4, Henry George Collection.

5. *Ibid.*

6. Barker, p. 24.

7. *Ibid.*, p. 52.

8. *Ibid.*, pp. 54-55.

9. Letters, 1854-1869, Henry George Collection. In passing a year or so earlier (April 18, [1860]), George also wrote to his sister about his state of mind: "It takes pretty much all my spare time to keep posted on the current topics of the day. What a time we live in, when great events follow one another so quickly that we have not space for wonder. We are driving at a killing pace somewhere—Emerson says to heaven, and Carlyle say[s] to the other place, but however much they differ, go we surely do."

10. Henry George, Jr., *The Life of Henry George* (New York: Schalkenbach Foundation Edition, 1960), p. 134.

11. *Ibid.*, p. 154.

12. See Melville's letter to Hawthorne (1? June 1851), *The Letters of Herman Melville,* ed. Merrell R. Davis and William H. Gilman (New Haven, 1960), pp. 130-31.

13. "On the Profitable Employment of Time" (March 25, 1865), in Henry George, Jr., pp. 157-58.

14. Barker, p. 68.

15. Henry George, Jr., p. 176.

16. Barker, pp. 97-98.

17. "What the Railroad Will Bring Us," in *The Papers Printed in "The Overland Monthly,"* 1868-71, Henry George Collection, pp. 302; 306. This essay is quoted at length in Henry George, Jr., pp. 177-79. Henry George, Jr., also quotes the whole of George's first letter on Lincoln, "Sic Semper Tyrannis!," pp. 162-64. See also manuscripts in Henry George Collection, especially for the editorial on Lincoln (typed copy).

Chapter Two

1. Barker, p. 123.
2. Barker, p. 124.
3. "The Chinese on the Pacific Coast," Henry George Scrap Books, Vol. XXI. See also pamphlet, Vol. III.
4. "Justice the Object—Taxation the Means," in *The Complete Works* (New York, 1906-11) VIII, 299.
5. Henry George, Jr., pp. 210-11.
6. Letters, 1883-84, Henry George Collection (typed copy).
7. *Henry George's 1886 Campaign*, ed. L. F. Post and F. C. Leubuscher (New York, [1961]), pp. 28-29.
8. Henry George, Jr., p. 210.
9. Letters, 1869-80, Henry George Collection. See also Henry George Scrap Books, III, 41.
10. Barker, p. 135.
11. San Francisco *Post,* editorial, April 7, 1873.
12. Sacramento *Reporter,* editorial, May 12, 1870.
13. San Francisco *Post,* editorial, April 16, 1874.
14. *Our Land and Land Policy,* V, 43. Pamphlet, Vol. III, Henry George Collection. This volume includes "The Chinese on the Pacific Coast," "The Subsidy Question . . ." (1871) and "Why Work is Scarce . . ." (1878). See also *Complete Works,* VIII, which includes "The Study of Political Economy," and VII, which includes "Moses." George's important addresses are also reprinted in pamphlet form by the Robert Schalkenbach Foundation.
15. *Ibid.,* III, p. 31.
16. See Chapter I for George's attitude toward Maximilian.
17. London *Times* editorial, September 6, 1882. Quoted in Elwood P. Lawrence, *Henry George in the British Isles* (East Lansing, Michigan, [1957]), pp. 25-26.

Chapter Three

1. September 15, 1879, Letters, 1869-80, Henry George Collection. Also Henry George, Jr., p. 321.
2. Henry George, Jr., pp. 322-23.
3. *The State,* I, 3 (April 18, 1879), 2. Henry George Collection.
4. George R. Geiger, Introduction, *The Philosophy of Henry George* (New York, 1933), p. x.
5. Barker, p. 267. See also Geiger, p. 80. George refers to other parts of Buckle's work. In fact, he takes Buckle to task for his Malthusian views. See *Progress and Poverty,* Bk. II, Ch. II, p. 115; Bk. III, Ch. II, p. 171.

6. The numbers in parentheses following any quotation in Section III of this chapter refer to the pagination in the standard edition of *Progress and Poverty* published by the Robert Schalkenbach Foundation.

7. Barker says that George did not use the phrase "the single tax" in print "with the definite article included" until 1885 (p. 444). "A single tax" appears in *Progress and Poverty.* See, for example, Bk. IX, Ch. I, p. 433.

8. Barker, pp. 294-95.

9. Quoted at greater length in Henry George, Jr., p. 323.

10. *Ibid.*, pp. 323-24.

11. January 26, 1880, Henry George Scrap Books, XXIV, p. 11.

12. February 21, 1880, *ibid.*, pp. 20-21.

13. March 27, 1880, *ibid.*, pp. 36-39. See also VIII, 29-30; 41-43; 44-45, for clippings from the Sacramento *Record-Union*, March 27, 1880, the date on which the paper printed George's reply.

14. February 1, 1880, *ibid.*, p. 15.

15. March 14, 1880, *ibid.*, pp. 30-33.

16. *Scribner's Monthly*, XXII (June, 1881), 312. Cf. New York *Herald*, Henry George Scrap Books, Vol. 8, p. 27.

17. Barker, pp. 318, 339.

18. A. N. Young, *The Single Tax Movement in the United States* (Princeton, 1916), p. 76.

19. Henry George Scrap Books, XXV-XXVI, pages unnumbered.

20. *Quarterly Review*, CLV (1883), 37.

21. *Edinburgh Review*, CLVII (1883), 290.

Chapter Four

1. The page references in parentheses throughout the chapter are once again to the readily accessible Schalkenbach Foundation editions of George's works.

2. Henry George, Jr., p. 409.

3. From Dublin, November 3, 1881. Letters to the *Irish World*, 1881-82, Henry George Scrap Books, XII.

4. Letter to Patrick Ford, Letters, 1881-82, Henry George Collection.

5. George's personal letters to Ford should be read as a gloss to his published dispatches. His frank appraisals of the men involved, like Parnell, are illuminating. See especially the four copy books in Letters, 1881-82, Henry George Collection.

6. See Elwood P. Lawrence, *Henry George in the British Isles*, Chapter 7 especially.

7. *Fortnightly Review*, XXXI, new series; XXXVII, old series (1882), 780-94. The article was entitled "England and Ireland: An American View" and was one of the sharpest, and strongest, that George ever wrote in the short essay form.

8. London, May 9, 1882. Letters to the *Irish World*, 1881-82.

9. Letter to Patrick Ford, Letters, 1881-82, Henry George Collection.

10. *Ibid.*

11. Henry George, Jr., p. 392.

12. *Ibid.*, p. 394.

13. Reprinted in the New York *World*, September 17, 1882—date-line Sept. 16th, when the letter was formally filed in Washington.

14. Letter to Hamlin Garland. See above, Chapter I, ln.

15. Henry George, Jr., p. 419.

16. See Barker, p. 397, for Ruskin's opinion of *Progress and Poverty*; see the London *Times*, January 2, 1884, quoted in Lawrence, p. 35, for Ruskin's note to George.

17. Henry George, Jr., p. 427.

18. Liverpool *Post* editorial quoted, *ibid.*, p. 430.

19. Barker, p. 404.

20. Lawrence, pp. 40-41. See Lawrence, Chapter IV, for a survey of George's speeches as recorded in British newspapers in 1884.

21. Henry George, Jr., p. 452.

22. Like many of George's important addresses, "The Crime of Poverty" is reprinted in pamphlet form by the Schalkenbach Foundation. See also the bound printed pamphlets in the Henry George Collection and *The Complete Works*, VIII, 185-218.

23. *The Complete Works*, VIII, 197. See p. 200 for a brief adaptation of the Robinson Crusoe passage from *Protection or Free Trade*.

24. *Ibid.*, p. 202.

Chapter Five

1. Interview in New York *Herald*, November 14, 1886, p. 8.

2. *Henry George's 1886 Campaign*, p. 3.

3. *Ibid.*, pp. 8-9.

4. September 10, 1886, Letters, 1885-1888, Henry George Collection.

5. *Henry George's 1886 Campaign*, p. 169.

6. *Ibid.*, p. 170.

7. Henry George, Jr., p. 463.

8. *Henry George's 1886 Campaign*, p. 169.

9. See Barker, pp. 479-81; 670.

10. "The United Labor Party and Socialism," editorial, *Standard*, August 13, 1887, p. 1. The complete file of the *Standard* is in the Henry George Collection. Unfortunately the file of the San Francisco *Post* is broken.

11. *Ibid.*

12. November 25, 1887, Letters, 1885-1888, Henry George Collection (typed copy).

13. Henry George, Jr., p. 552.

14. See James J. Green, *The Impact of Henry George's Theories on American Catholics* (Ph.D. thesis, University of Notre Dame, 1956).

15. Henry George, Jr., p. 385.

16. *Standard*, "A Statement from Dr. M'Glynn," February 5, 1887, p. 1. On the front page of the *Standard*, McGlynn quoted the correspondence between the Archbishop and himself.

17. *Ibid.*, June 25, 1887, p. 1. For an important editorial on the case during the previous winter, see, for example, *ibid.*, January 8, 1887.

18. Henry George, Jr., p. 495.

19. *Ibid.*, p. 562.

20. December 23, 1892, Letters, 1891-June 1893, Henry George Collection (typed copy). The letter was written in answer to one of Dawson's, dated December 14, 1892, New Priory, Quex Road, London, N.W., in which Dawson thanked George for promising him a copy of *A Perplexed Philosopher*. He said he would be "sure to enjoy it even more than the letter to Leo XIII." He also said of Bishop Nulty's silence on the letter to the Pope: "Possibly he may however have felt a delicacy about acknowledging the Pope's bad arguments or misapprehensions." George always had his sympathizers within the Church.

21. Henry George, Jr., p. 565. See Henry George, Jr.'s letter to his father (May 30, 1891) for his immediate reactions. Letters, 1891-June, 1893, Henry George Collection.

22. *Ibid.*, p. 565.

23. *Ibid.*, p. 567.

24. To James E. Mills, May 18, 1891, Letters, 1891-June, 1893, Henry George Collection. On the same day, George wrote to Father Dawson, apologizing for the long delay in their correspondence and explaining his recuperation from illness in Bermuda. Thanking Dawson for his support, he said, "I very much appreciate the value of your support, although I do not wish in any way to embarrass you. But it is very sad to see the general tendency on the part of all clergymen—and it is quite as marked, perhaps even more so, among the Protestant sects even to the Unitarian—to avoid the simple principle of justice. As Tolstoi has put it, they are willing to do anything for the poor except to get off their backs. This is leading them into the advocacy of socialism and to all sorts of dangerous things, even to the acceptance and even advocacy of principles which will lead ultimately to atheism. Nor do I believe that anything is to be hoped from the papal encyclical. If I can judge from what has been printed of it, it will have the same characteristics." George soon found his assumptions to be correct; he also anticipated some of the arguments he was to use.

25. *Standard*, editorial, March 2, 1889, p. 1.

26. From Russell Square, London, March 8, 1889. Letters, 1889-1890, Henry George Collection. Webb wrote to welcome George, referring to his conversations with him in New York City before the 1888 elections, and to inform him "about the state of affairs here." He said, "What holds things back is the great mass of middle class, religious, 'respectable,' cautious & disliking the Radical artisan. These need your instruction most. . . ." Webb's observation really described those to whom George would appeal in the future and the success he would have "in stirring up the *bourgeoisie*—especially among dissenting sects." Webb's estimations of George are generally sound.

27. Quoted in Henry George, Jr., p. 514. See Rollin Sawyer's *Henry George and the Single Tax* for a series of entries (articles, reviews, interviews) in which Tolstoy praised and defended George's views.

28. *Standard*, August 31, 1889, p. 1.

29. *The Complete Works*, VIII, 303. See Chapter 2, 4n and 14n, especially for a note on George's pamphlets currently in print.

30. May 17, 1890. Letters, 1829-1890, Henry George Collection. See Chapter III, 10n.

31. Henry George, Jr., pp. 599-600.

32. *Ibid.*, pp. 605-6. See *The Flushing Journal*, October 30, 1897, Henry George Collection (Henry George Jr., Letters, 1882-1916). Henry George, Jr., was preparing his biography of his father in the years immediately following his death. The son's papers contain many interesting items sent to him by those who knew Henry George and whom he could contact at the time.

33. *Ibid.*, p. 604.

34. Cf., for example, *A Perplexed Philosopher*, p. 136.

35. Henry George, Jr., p. 589.

36. *Yale Review*, VII (August, 1898), 231. That Barker should concur generally with Hadley's assessment—after judiciously quoting most of this same brief review—may come as a surprise to anyone interested in George's efforts for social reform. Hadley's motives and commitment to the very things that moved earlier hostile reviewers (Hadley is obviously hostile) should not go without remark (see Barker, pp. 583-87). Hadley's irony is occasionally but unintentionally correct. The second sentence on *Progress and Poverty* is a good example of ironic praise: Hadley may not think much of a book on political economy that sermonizes, but irony aside one could not argue with the statement. *Progress and Poverty* is, indeed, "one of the most eloquent volumes of sermons which has appeared in the English language." *The Science of Political Economy* is often just as eloquent as its famous predecessor. Hadley gives himself away. The so-called "commonplace metaphysics" of the posthumous book is the very same that helped to make *Progress and Poverty* the success it was and the singular book it will always be. Hadley's praise is what William Blake would call a "Grecian Mock."

37. New York *Journal*, November 2, 1896. Henry George Scrap Books, V, 60-61. See p. 61 in particular. See also p. 89.

38. *Ibid.* The series in the *Journal* began at convention time with the July 4, 1896, issue which carried George's article, "The New Line in Our Politics."

Chapter Six

1. One of the honorary pallbearers was Robert Schalkenbach whose will made possible the foundation which keeps George's works in print.

2. See the Henry George Scrap Books, especially VI, VII, XXI, XXVII for public reaction and the Correspondence of Henry George, Jr., and Mrs. George for personal messages of condolence, Henry George Collection.

3. Samuel Gompers, *Seventy Years of Life and Labor* (New York, 1925) I, 313, 316. See also Peter A. Speek, *The Single Tax and the Labor Movement* (Madison, Wisconsin, 1917).

4. *Saturday Review*, LXXXIV (November 6, 1897), 485-86.

5. *Labor Echo*, November 6, 1897.

6. "The Influence of Henry George," *Fortnightly Review*, LXII, news series (1897), 843-44.

7. Quoted in "Count Tolstoi on the Doctrine of Henry George," *Ameri-*

can *Monthly Review of Reviews*, XVII (1898), 73. In a letter to Henry George, Jr. (November 14, 1909), an acquaintance wrote: "Some 3 or 4 years ago, a customer of mine, a Mr. Mandelkern went to visit Tolstoy for the N.Y. Times, as soon [as] he was introduced to him as coming from N.Y. Tolstoy's first question was about the single tax and the children of H. G. Mandelkern had to confess he knew little about either of them, but told his barber was a great H. G. man. Whereupon Tolstoy answered, 'well if he understands the single tax, he is a greater man than your president Roosevelt, even if he is only a barber.'" Henry George, Jr., Letters, 1881-1916, Henry George Collection.

8. Letter to E. H. Crosby of New York, a single-taxer, reprinted in the *Clarion*, October 16, 1897.

9. "Count Tolstoi on the Doctrine of Henry George," p. 74.

10. See the New York *Times*, September 9, 1928, Section 10, p. 6, for an article by Count Ilya Tolstoy which supports what I have called Tolstoy's "American consciousness" and indicates the interest he had in the works and acts of Emerson, Thoreau, William Lloyd Garrison, and George.

11. For single-tax activity from George's death to 1916, see A. N. Young, *The Single Tax Movement in the United States*.

12. For a review of the Fels Fund activity, see Young, *The Single Tax Movement in the United States*.

13. The school obviously helped to fill the need for thoughtful social protest in the depression-ridden 1930's. Oscar Geiger had worked for Henry George's election in 1897, knew him personally, and attended the twenty-fifth anniversary dinner of 1905. Along with other well-known social reformers who accepted special invitations in 1905, including the speakers, were Clarence Darrow, Lincoln Steffens, and Ida Tarbell.

14. The Schalkenbach Foundation occupies space in the New York headquarters of the Henry George School of Social Science.

15. See also, Markham's "The Right to Labor in Joy." George will always have a place in the literature of protest, even if his influence is only general. Typed copies of the poems are in the papers of Henry George, Jr., Henry George Collection. See Walter F. Taylor, *The Economic Novel in America* (Chapel Hill, 1942).

16. Barker, p. 621.

17. *Ibid.*, pp. 634-35.

18. *Ibid.*, p. 631.

19. Letter to Henry George, Jr., from Dublin, January 7, 1882. Henry George, Jr., Letters, 1881-1916, Henry George Collection.

20. New York *Times*, October 2, 1881. The poem was clipped and sent to George by Mrs. Lowell, Francis Shaw's daughter and the daughter-in-law of the poet.

Selected Bibliography

PRIMARY SOURCES

1. *Henry George Collection*:

   The major collection of Henry George's published and unpublished works, manuscripts, scrapbooks, notebooks, lectures, correspondence, including bibliographies and related material, is housed in the New York Public Library. A catalogue of this collection, published in 1926, is *Henry George and the Single Tax* by Rollin Alger Sawyer, then chief of the Economics Division of the library.

2. *Standard Editions*:

   The Writings of Henry George. Ed. HENRY GEORGE, JR. 10 vols. Memorial Edition. New York: Doubleday and McClure, 1898-1901.

   The Complete Works of Henry George. 10 vols. Fels Fund Library Edition. Garden City, New York: Doubleday, Page & Co., 1906-1911.

   Volume 10 of *The Writings* and Volumes 9 and 10 of *The Complete Works* include *The Life of Henry George* by Henry George, Jr.

3. *Selected Condensations of "Progress and Poverty"* (all available through the Robert Schalkenbach Foundation):

   Henry George's "Progress and Poverty." A new and condensed edition. Ed. A. W. MADSEN. London: Hogarth Press, 1966 (first issued, 1953).

   Progress and Poverty by Henry George. Rearranged and abridged for modern readers. Ed. H. G. BROWN. New York: Schalkenbach, 1951 (first issued, 1940).

   More Progress and Less Poverty. Ed. J. S. THOMPSON. New York: Schalkenbach, 1942.

   Progress and Poverty. (Condensed.) Ed. J. L. BUSEY. New York: Schalkenbach, n.d. These condensations are listed in order of increased brevity. Like all abridgements, they damage unavoidably the literary and poetic character of George's book.

   All of Henry George's major works and many of his minor writings have been reprinted by the Robert Schalkenbach Foundation, New York City. The Foundation is associated with the Henry George School of Social Science, branches of which are located throughout the world; therefore, George's works are always in print. These include *Progress and Poverty, Social Problems, Protection or Free Trade, The Land Question, Etc., A Perplexed Philosopher, The Science of Political Economy*; a selection of his shorter writings in pamphlet form; *Henry George's 1886 Campaign*, prepared by L. F. Post and F. C. Leubuscher (a collection of important speeches by George and others); *The Life of Henry George* by his son; and a *Concordance to Progress and Poverty*, compiled by H. M. McEvoy.

Selected Bibliography

SECONDARY SOURCES

Selected Biography and Criticism:

BARKER, CHARLES A. *Henry George.* New York: Oxford University Press, 1955. Fundamentally a biography, this book attempts the most complete over-all assessment of George.

COLEMAN, MCALISTER. *Pioneers of Freedom.* Intro. NORMAN THOMAS. New York: Vanguard Press, 1929. Includes a section on George—mainly introductory.

CORD, STEVEN B. *Henry George: Dreamer or Realist?* Philadelphia: University of Pennsylvania Press [1965]. Surveys and assesses reactions of economists and historians to George from 1879 to 1964. Good bibliography. (This study was published after I completed my book.)

DE MILLE, ANNA GEORGE. *Henry George, Citizen of the World.* Ed. DON C. SHOEMAKER. Chapel Hill, North Carolina: University of North Carolina Press [1950]. A personalized biographical appreciation by George's daughter—especially valuable for its intimacy.

DOMBROWSKI, JAMES. "Henry George: A Prophet of Social Justice." *The Early Days of Christian Socialism in America.* New York: Columbia University Press, 1936. Pp. 35-49. Places George among Christian Socialists.

EDWARDS, HERBERT. "Herne, Garland, and Henry George," *American Literature,* XXVIII (1956), 359-67. Examines George's influence in his own time on younger writers whose interest in economics was not their primary concern.

ELY, RICHARD T. *The Labor Movement in America.* New York: Macmillan, 1905. Includes significant references to George.

GEIGER, GEORGE R. "The Forgotten Man: Henry George," *Antioch Review,* I (1941), 291-307. A valuable introduction in retrospect.

————. *The Philosophy of Henry George.* Intro. JOHN DEWEY. New York: Macmillan, 1933. Fullest discussion of George's ideas.

GEORGE, HENRY, JR. *The Life of Henry George.* 2 vols. New York: Doubleday, Page & Co., 1911. The first and in some ways the best survey of George's varied life—includes many quotations from unpublished documents, other less accessible sources, family reminiscences, and personal conversations.

HOBSON, J. A. "The Influence of Henry George," *Fortnightly Review,* LXII n.s. (1897), 835-44. A generally fair, valuable contemporary review from a non-Georgist perspective of George's impact at the end of the nineteenth century.

HUXLEY, THOMAS H. "Capital—the Mother of Labour," *Nineteenth Century,* XXVII (1890), 513-32. Records Huxley's hostile attitude to George's ideas and influence.

LAWRENCE, ELWOOD P. *Henry George in the British Isles.* East Lansing, Michigan: Michigan State University Press [1957]. Fullest study of George's influence and activities in England, Scotland, and Ireland. Supplements Henry George, Jr., Geiger, and Barker.

MACKENDRICK, ALEXANDER. "Henry George's Teaching," *Westminster Review*, CLXXII (1912), 133-42. Early serious review of historical value.

MADISON, CHARLES A. "Henry George, Prophet of Human Rights," *South Atlantic Quarterly*, XLIII (1944), 349-60. Essentially introductory but with valuable insights.

NOBLE, RANSOM E. "Henry George and the Progressive Movement," *American Journal of Economics and Sociology*, VIII (1949), 259-69. Brief survey of George's influence on American progressive political leaders from 1900 to 1930, including Bryan, La Follette, Theodore Roosevelt, and Wilson.

NOCK, ALBERT J. *Henry George: An Essay*. New York: Morrow [1939]. A standard account by an interesting writer.

POST, LOUIS F. *Taxation and Land Value*. 5th Edition. Indianapolis, Indiana: Bobbs-Merrill [1915]. Important general review by a co-worker of George.

————. *The Prophet of San Francisco: Personal Memories and Interpretations of Henry George*. Chicago: L. S. Dickey & Co., [1904]; New York: Vanguard [1930]. Contains many important, valuable reminiscences.

SPEEK, PETER A. *The Single Tax and the Labor Movement*. Bulletin of the University of Wisconsin, No. 878. Economics and Political Science Series, VIII, 3, 247-426. Madison, Wisconsin: University of Wisconsin Press, 1917. A good review of the dialogue between the Single Taxers and the Labor Movement.

SPENCER, HERBERT. "Unpublished Letters . . . , the Henry George Controversy," *Independent*, LVI (1904), 1169-74; 1471-78. Reveals Spencer's attitude towards George. Important to George's *A Perplexed Philosopher*.

TARBELL, IDA M. "New Dealers of the Seventies," *Forum*, XCII (1934), 133-39. Valuable for its historical perspective from the depression-ridden 1930's on George as a precursor of the New Deal.

TAYLOR, WALTER F. *The Economic Novel in America*. Chapel Hill, North Carolina: University of North Carolina Press, 1942. Includes a section on George's relation to the thesis novel.

TEILHAC, ERNEST. *Pioneers of American Economic Thought in the Nineteenth Century*. Tr. E. A. J. JOHNSON. New York: Macmillan, 1936. Includes a chapter on George in a helpful survey of early American economists—mainly introductory.

TOYNBEE, ARNOLD. *"Progress and Poverty," a Criticism of Mr. Henry George*. London: Kegan Paul, 1883. Records Toynbee's disturbed, hostile reaction to George; states essentially the case for the Establishment at the time of George's greatest impact on the social, political, and economic life of the United Kingdom.

YOUNG, ARTHUR N. *The Single Tax Movement in the United States*. Princeton, New Jersey: Princeton University Press, 1916. Early but still very valuable survey of George's relation to the Single Tax movement and its subsequent development—includes many quotations from important editorials.

Index

This index is limited to important items in the text, but also includes a selection of references to significant persons and subjects in the Notes. It does not include items in the Chronology.